Christian Belief for Today

Attempts from different points of view

Rainer Stahl

Copyright © 2022 Rainer Stahl
Copyright © 2022 Generis Publishing

All rights reserved. This book or any portion thereof may not be reproduced or used in any manner whatsoever without the written permission of the publisher except for the use of brief quotations in a book review.

Title: Christian Belief for Today

Attempts from different points of view

ISBN: 979-8-88676-046-0

Author: Rainer Stahl

Cover image: www.pixabay.com

Publisher: Generis Publishing
Online orders: www.generis-publishing.com
Contact email: info@generis-publishing.com

Table of Contents

Preface 3

Christian Belief for Today 5

God offers Peace – a more than 2.600 Years old Conviction of Faith 21

"God has made everything beautiful" 27

Do exist Messianic Texts in our Old Testament? 30

First Easter, then Christmas 47

"I will make a covenant of peace with them" 53

Jesus Christ is the true Sun 57

"You are right, Teacher" 62

The sixth supplication of the Lord's Prayer 66

Martin Luther as Translator of the Bible 77

Martin Luther as Poet of Hymns 90

Even for us Christians: no picture for God! 111

"You shall live!" 116

Jonah 2, Meditation for the Workshop of Sermons of the Luther-Convent in the Evangelical Church in the Rhineland 120

Scriptures Index 126

Index of Illustrations 127

Preface

It was really a challenging question as from the publishing house "Generis Publishing" the request came, whether I could publish my paper about the sixth supplication of the Lord's Prayer, which I had already published in the year 2020 in Saint Petersburg, in a new publication of this publishing house. A prolongation – maybe as work about all supplications of the Lord's Prayer – was in the moment not possible for me. But it was given to me the hint, to collect several papers which I already had written into one new volume. To take this chance I liked very much. It shows clearly the task of "Generis Publishing": It "is especially designed for worldwide authors, to make every publishing experience the best it can be" – as it is written in the homepage of this publishing house.

I have collected texts, which I had translated into English, because I hoped that I could give them in parishes in Russia, or which I had given there already. In English because my colleague in Tscheboksary is very fluid in this language. And I'm able to document Bible quotes in Russian language more in a passive way. Therefore, I have taken the presently most important papers for me and united them in this volume:

> A paper about aspects of the Christian Belief today,
> a paper about the question whether we may identify messianic texts
> in the Old Testament,
> then the paper about the Lord's Prayer,
> and two papers about Martin Luther:
> In the 500th year of the German translation of the Bible a paper about his work as
> translator of the Bible, and a paper about him as writer of hymns, as poet.

In between of these papers I have added some sermons: First sermons which are already prepared in English for the visit of parishes in Russia and recently written sermons which I had to translate especially into English.

I'm very much hoping, that this volume will find persons who are interested in these texts. It might be of interest, why I'm able to do this work: From 1998 to 2016 I could have served as General Secretary of the Martin-Luther-Bund, of the Martin Luther Association. This is the Lutheran diaspora association in Germany, which is connected to the United Evangelical-Lutheran Church in Germany and to the German National Committee of the Lutheran World Federation. This work had given me the possibility to serve many diaspora churches mainly in Eastern Europe. During this work I also came into touch with congregations in Russia, with whom even now in my time of retirement good connections are possible.

Therefore, at the end of this preface I have to underline my wish, that between the Ukraine and Russia very soon peace will be possible: That "God offers peace" (Numbers 6:26) also for all people in this region! That God "will make a covenant of peace with them" (Ezekiel 37:26).

Rainer Stahl, Erlangen, Easter 2022.

Christian Belief for Today.
Some Thoughts to its Strengthening[1]

1. Introduction

"Even progressive Christians of today have to be conservative otherwise they would be no Christians any more. What Christianity makes important are defined by the biblical revelation, the experience of faith, the tradition and the church."[2]

Whom I might have quoted? I do not think that you may imagine the name of the author but his spiritual and theological connection: The combination of "biblical revelation, the experience of faith, the tradition and the church" shows us, how to answer my question:

Even we evangelical Lutheran Christians live in connections: Even we need the church, even we live in a certain tradition, even we need a certain experience of faith. But we say that only the fundamental decisions have importance for us: "Christ alone", "Scripture alone". Now we may imagine from whom the quote in the beginning is: from a roman-catholic colleague. I have chosen this quote because it's also important to understand what makes us unique: If we as Christians want to be progressive, we have to be conservative in a good sense.

The author has additionally written: "The Christians of today have to be conservative in a critical and discerning way: to enlighten the enlighteners, to emancipate the emancipators, to criticize the criticizers. [...] And when they try to work as »salt of the earth«, they first should turn around and start by themselves."[3] In this spiritual behavior I want to grasp some impulses and pass them on to you.

---

[1] This text was written in 2012 as preparation of lectures in Latvia and Slovenia. But because of personal reasons these trips never have taken place. For this paper the text was actualized and adapted to the present time.
[2] Cf.: Wolfgang Ockenfels: Das hohe C. Wohin steuert die CDU, Augsburg 2009, p. 153f.
[3] Op. cit., p. 156.

2. The Holy Spirit creates the relation to God

2.1.
«И сказал Моисей Богу:	"Then Moses said to God,
вот я прийду к сынам Израилевым	If I come to the people of Israel
и скажу им:	and say to them,
"Бог отцов наших послал	»The God of your fathers has sent
меня к вам".	me to you«,
А они скажут мне:	and they ask me,
"как ему имя?"	»What is his name?«
Что сказать мне им?	what shall I say to them?
Бог сказал Моисею:	God said to Moses,
אֶהְיֶה אֲשֶׁר אֶהְיֶה / Я БУДУ КОТОРЫЙ Я БУДУ	I AM WHO I AM.
И сказал:	And he said,
так скажи сынам Израилевым:	Say this to the people of Israel,
"Я БУДУ послал меня к вам"»	»I AM has sent me to you«
(Исход / Exodus 3:13-14).	

Moses is asking God how he should speak about God in front of the Israelites. He would like to have a name, a formula, which identifies God. And God is answering – like it is in Hebrew – with three words: Two times the identical term – the first person singular of the verb "to be" – אֶהְיֶה – and in between of them the Hebrew word which means "what is" or "who" – אֲשֶׁר. The form of the verb "to be" means an activity, which is going on, means something, what has started. It means something what is not concluded but continues into the future. Because of that we should translate in a future form: «Я буду» / "I will be". This means: God's activities continue always into the future, that we can trust on them.

This is the first insight we can have from this Bible word: "I AM WHO I AM" shows the work of the Holy Spirit. Only as gift of the Holy Spirit I can believe that God is always near to me!

2.2. May be most of you have heard about Dietrich Bonhoeffer. He was involved into the opposition against Adolf Hitler and his terroristic and unjust system. On April 5th of 1943 he was arrested. Two years later he was sentenced to death and murdered in the concentration camp Flossenbürg on April 9th 1945. The Church of England has honored him as one of the "Martyrs of the 20th century": Since 1998 his statue is on Westminster Abbey in London. Even the Romanian

Orthodox Church witnesses him as martyr: In its cathedral in Nuremberg he is one of the "Confessors of Christ" on a painted live tree.[4]

Bonhoeffer has formulated in letters from the prison the following theses for his time and the future: "We're entering into a time totally free of any kind of religion; the people, as they are, cannot be any more religious. Even those who declare themselves honestly »religious« do not practice this [...]."[5] "The Pauline question, whether the περιτομή [the circumcision] is necessary for justification sounds today – as I think – whether religion would be a reason for salvation. The liberation from circumcision [...] is also liberation from religion [...]"[6] – as he has formulated it in a letter from April 30th of 1944.

Two months later – in a letter from June 27th of 1944 – he added the following insights: "Presently I'm writing the interpretation of the Ten Commandments. Especially the first is difficult for me. The traditional interpretation of the service of gods, of idols as a service of »richness, sexuality and honor« seems to be not really biblical. That's moralizing. The prayer to gods has as reason that people at least pray to someone. But we do not pray anymore, even not to gods. We are really nihilists."[7]

2.3. Bonhoeffer had referred to the tradition of interpreting of the First Commandment – that it would exclude the service of idols. There we can remember Martin Luther! I give some sentences of his interpretation in the Large Catechism from April 1529:

"What means: to have a God or what is God? Answer: God means that of whom we expect all good [...]. Therefore: To have a God is nothing else than to trust and believe in him [...]. Only trust and faith of the heart creates both: God and idol. Whether faith and trust are correct then also your God is correct. [...] That's because faith and God belong together: Where are you trusting in – that is your God [...].
Some are feeling that they would have enough when they have money and goods. [...] Look, they also have a god, which is called »Mammon«, that is money and goods [...].

---

[4] Grigore and Maria Popescu (Ed.): Catedrala Ortodoxa Romana / Rumänische Orthodoxe Kathedrale: Nürnberg. Fresca și istorie / Freskenmalerei und Geschichte, Cluj-Napoca 2009, p. 196.200.
[5] Cf.: Christus für uns heute. Eine Bonhoeffer-Auswahl, selected by Walter Schultz, Berlin 1970, p. 335 (translation into English from myself).
[6] Op. cit., p. 336 (translation into English from myself).
[7] Op. cit., p. 344f (translation into English from myself).

But also who trusts in knowledge, relationship and honor has a God, but not the correct one. [...]
Therefore, I'm again saying that this would be the correct interpretation of this commandment: To have a God means to have something where you can totally trust in [...].
Now you understand very easy what this commandment requires: To invest the whole heart in God alone! [...]."[8]

Martin Luther lived in a much more religious time and society than Bonhoeffer or we. But he does not think of a natural religiosity. Luther explains that we could keep to totally worldly things – to pray to nothing, as Bonhoeffer said in the 20th century –, but within that to make things to a God! Martin Luther would have said: Nihilists in the sense that we trust in nothing – this we cannot do. As people we have to trust in something. Only, as long we trust in something, we remain to be people!

Here I have to explain something: I have identified "being religious" and "trust in something". May be through this way I have shown that I'm a Lutheran! "Religiosity" might have many different aspects. But without "trust" I cannot think of that.

2.4. But this trust always is under discussion. It can be directed to something wrong. We have the task to orient it to the correct thing! I again look into the Large Catechism: "Look, what we have done in the blindness under the Pope: Had a person a problem with a tooth he prayed to the holy Apolonia [and so on] [...]. They all have put their heart and trust to others than on the true God."[9]

The meaning of the biblical message is as follows: That the spirit of God takes our trust and directs it to the true God! To this we only can invite. We all bring natural circumstances with us – also the ability to trust. But to trust in the true God, this means a change we only can do under the guidance of the Holy Spirit: «Верующий в него не постыдится» / "He who believes will not be in haste" (Исаия / Isaiah 28:16б/b)!

2.5. The biologist Eckart Voland says it in the following way: "For sure: There are no genes for one or the other of the thousands of religions. [...] But there are

---

[8] Die Bekenntnisschriften der evangelisch-lutherischen Kirche, Göttingen 1955, 2nd Edition, p. 560-563 (translation by myself).
[9] Op. cit. (like note: 8), p. 562 (translation by myself).

findings, which show a biological function of piety. For example: That those can deal in a better way with problems in their lives, which have a stabile worldview because they believe."[10]

It seems that Dietrich Bonhoeffer was not right, as he had imagined a world without religions. It seems that we need at least a kind of religiosity.[11] But then is not defined in what cultural relations we live our "born" religiosity – whether we find our home in religious communities, whether we find the relation to the true God. The most common realization of religiosity is to go to concerts of famous bands and to honor Pop-Icons,[12] is the membership of Fan-Groups of soccer-gamers. The first "churches", or better: sanctuaries of our time are the sport-arenas and the concert-halls. I remember a photo about the Petrowskij-Stadion in the book «Санкт Петербург. Сутки напролёт» / "St. Petersburg. Around the clock": «В сегодняшнем мире любовь к футболу сродни религии» – „Today being a soccer fun is next to a religion".[13]

2.6. But – and this is the real challenge of our time, which Bonhoeffer and Luther could not have seen – the modern research is able to identify many natural, inner worldly reasons for our behavior and our life. My thesis is as follows: When we look to our religious experiences with our natural sense we only can grasp those aspects which are open to our human and worldly view. We only can realize the "materializing aspects". But this does not mean that aspects beyond of our world would not exist. But into these aspects we cannot just look and go. Those aspects only the Spirit of God can open to us – that's the position in the Bible and in our Lutheran tradition.[14]

---

[10] Eckart Voland: Warum sind Menschen religiös?, FOCUS 11/2010, p. 78 (translation by myself).
[11] Vgl. Edgar Thaidigsmann: »Religiös unmusikalisch« Aspekte einer hermeneutischen Problematik, ZThK 108, 2011, p. 490-509: „Doch ist damit weder ein verbreitetes Bedürfnis zu glauben verschwunden, wenngleich es vielfach sich in profaner Gestalt darstellt, noch ist der christliche Glaube theologisch dadurch schon in die Freiheit zu seiner Sache gebracht [...]" (p. 507).
[12] See a fate which many has moved: G. Czöppan, H.J. Hohl, N. Waldenmaier: Fall einer Göttin, FOCUS 8/2012, p. 92f (zu Whitney Houston).
[13] Санкт Петербург. Сутки напролёт / St. Petersburg. Around the clock, St. Petersburg 2011, p. 204-205. Perhaps better: „being a soccer fan".
[14] Cf. Edgar Thaidigsmann, op. cit. (like note: 11), p. 507: „[...] muss die Theologie sich auf das Besondere des in der ursprünglichen Überlieferung wirksamen Geistes besinnen, dem sich der christliche Glaube verdankt."

3. God the Almighty governs all life

3.1. Now I have to come back to the important statement in Исход / Exodus 3:

«Бог сказал Моисею:	"God said to Moses,
אֶהְיֶה אֲשֶׁר אֶהְיֶה / Я БУДУ КОТОРЫЙ Я БУДУ	I AM WHO I AM.
И сказал:	And he said,
так скажи сынам Израилевым:	Say this to the people of Israel,
"Я БУДУ послал меня к вам"	"I AM has sent me to you"
(Исход / Exodus 3:14).	

From the middle of the third century before Christ Jewish theologians have translated the holy texts into the Greek language – first the Torah, which means also our passage. They have written for these three Hebrew words – אֶהְיֶה אֲשֶׁר אֶהְיֶה – four Greek words: First the word for the first person singular: "εγω" – in Russian: «я». Then the verb "to be" in that person: "ειμι" – in Russian: «есмь». And finally the defining word "ο ών" – in your Russian bible you have an old form of «есть»: «Сущий»:

«Бог сказал Моисею:	"God said to Moses,
"Я есмь Сущий."	»**I am the Being.**«
И сказал:	And he said,
так скажи сынам Израилевым:	Say this to the people of Israel,
"**Сущий** послал меня к вам."»	»**The Being** has sent me to you.«"

That's also a way for understanding of God: He is the really "Being". All what we see, all what we are, this all is only because God has called it, has called us into being. The really "Being" – are not we, but the really "Being" – that's God.

3.2. All who try to fight against our faith, who think they would have falsified our faith, they all do nothing than to lead us to "the God of the Gaps". And this God is only important for all who have no understanding and no explanations any more.

Also with this challenge Dietrich Bonhoeffer has dealt in 1944. At the end of his letter from April 30th he wrote: "The religious people speak of God when human knowledge or power is at end. It's always the »deus ex machina« / »the God out of the engine«. And when people push their borders a little bit forward, then this »deus ex machina« becomes a little bit more unimportant. [...] But I do not want to have God at the borders of life, I want to have him in the midst of life, not in the weakness but in the power, not only in the case of death and guilt but also in the case of life and good of the people."[15]

I also could say it in the following way: this "God of the Gaps" is a product of our own activities. He is – like Luther has called it – our idol we trust in, but not the God of the Bible, whom Christ is proclaiming us, from whom we have our whole life.

I have discussed my thoughts together with the rector of the theological seminary of the Federation of the Evangelical Lutheran Churches in Russia and other States in Saint Petersburg, Dr. Anton Tikhomirov. He says: «Для меня, например, Бог – это Тайна. Тайна как таковая, Тайна по определению. Бог – это бесконечная Тайна. Не потому, что мы ещё чего-то не знаем в силу ограниченности наших способностей, а потому что мы в принципе не способны познать, понять, воспринять и принять её. В любой тайне – отсвет Божественного. Там, где Тайна, там Бог».[16] / "For me God is also a mystery. A mystery as such. A mystery of definition. God is an endless mystery. Not because we do not yet know something because of our limited abilities, but because we are generally not in the situation to understand it, to grasp it, to agree with it. Each mystery has something divine. Where there is a mystery there is God."

When I understand God from the term mystery, «тайна», then I can grasp that all my life is carried from this mystery, «от эта тайна». Isn't this a behavior which we may understand as "trust"?

3.3.1. I draw your attention to a very special text: Luke 13:1-5 – the discussion about the fate of the Galileans who have been murdered by the Romans and the 18 citizens of Jerusalem who have been killed by the tower in Siloam. Jesus asked: «Или думаете ли, что [они] [...] виновнее были всех живущих в Иерусалиме?» / "Or [...] do you think that they that they were worse offenders [...] in Jerusalem?" (Verse 4).

---

[15] Op. cit. (like note: 5), p. 337 (translation by myself).
[16] «Я общаюсь с Вечностью через музыку» / „Ich habe Gemeinschaft mit der Ewigkeit durch die Musik" [...], in: Der Bote / Вестник 3-4/2011, p. 28-35, quote: p. 30. On p. 31 in German Language: „Für mich zum Beispiel ist Gott Geheimnis. Geheimnis an sich, Geheimnis per definitionem. Gott ist ein endloses Geheimnis. Nicht weil wir etwas wegen unserer begrenzten Fähigkeiten noch nicht wissen, sondern weil wir prinzipiell nicht in der Lage sind, es zu erkennen, zu begreifen, wahrzunehmen und anzunehmen. Jedes Geheimnis hat etwas Göttliches an sich. Wo Geheimnis ist, ist Gott."

Here Jesus is arguing in contrary to our thinking of an idol. We use such an idol to strengthen us against others. They are victims. Because of that they are guilty for us. And because of that God had let them dying. Through this way God becomes our idol for declaring others as guilty. Even Josephus, former priest and offspring of a high priestly family is blaming others but never his own priestly group. But Jesus told us to accept the solidarity of guilt: «но если не покаетесь, все так же погибкете» / "No; but unless you repent you will all likewise perish" (Verse 3).

3.3.2. A similar happening of our time: a Saturday, 4 o'clock 44 minutes p.m., Hamburg-Eppendorf: Persons who had been shopping or wanted to buy something for the weekend were waiting at a corner for green. But what came was the death. A car, too quick, rushed into the group and killed four persons. One couple, whose car was hit by this quick car was injured. The driver of the first car was under drugs. One of the killed persons, Günther Amendt, had published a best seller about the liberation of sexuality and had used drugs very frequently in his life. Together with Günther Amendt died the famous actor Dietmar Mues and his wife Sibylle. They had been well acquainted with the injured couple Peter Striebeck and his wife Ulla since long time.

This all might be a coincidence. Or we could ask for a meaning, like one time Thornton Wilder in a novel was speaking about "the perfect laboratory of God".[17]

3.3.3. Do we realize the difference? Our atheistic newspapers often write: "Where you have been – God?" There they explain a religiosity of their own. And they also express their feeling in a kind the longing for mystery – as Brother Tihkomirov had said. But not yet really in a Christian way!

Jesus, as we have learned from the gospel of Luke, does not interpret the things. He says to us: Do not try to understand the happenings of Galilee, of Jerusalem, of Hamburg-Eppendorf... And then he opens the message which we can find within those happenings for us: We should turn to new life, to real faith! We should not try to "understand" the "laboratory of God", but we should live each day our life under God. We should not be visitors, like those who take their mobile telephones and tablets and take photos of accidents. But we should be moved. We should change our life! Like it's explained in the book of Jeremiah:

---

[17] Cf.: Helmut Markwort: Das Leben schrieb ein dramatisches Drehbuch, FOCUS 12/2011, p. 66.

«Если хочешь обратится, Израиль, говорит Господь, ко Мне обратись» (Иеремия / Jeremiah 4:1).	"If you return, O Israel, says the Lord, to me you should return"

3.4. Now again I want to listen to Martin Luther. He makes a distinction between the hidden and the revealed God.[18] May I use this distinction in the following way: When we try to speak about God in a neutral way, when we try to look into his "laboratory" then we will not receive an answer or we will receive an answer we never can agree with. Then God is hiding himself. But when we ask for the revealed God then we will find ourselves like in a "space" of solving of our questions. What might it be – that "space"? What might it be – the revealed side of God? For Martin Luther it was Jesus Christ – his life and death in Judah in the first years of our time and his life and power now as resurrected one![19] Therefore we now have to ask directly after Jesus Christ.

4. Jesus Christ – the picture of God for us

4.1.
«И явился ему Ангел Господень в пламени огня из среды тернового куста. И увидел он, что терновый куст горит огнем, но куст не сгорает» (Исход / Exodus 3:2).	"And the angel of the Lord appeared to him in a flame of fire out of the midst of a bush; and he looked, and lo, the bush was burning, yet it was not consumed"

In the church of the middle age in western and central Europe and also in the church of the orthodoxy of today there exists a surprising interpretation of "this angel of the Lord in the flame of fire out of the midst of the bush, which was not consumed": Mary together with Christ as a child. This means: The "angel of the Lord" is Christ himself before his incarnation, therefore painted within the body of his mother.
Grigore and Maria Popescu have painted a fresco in the cathedral of the Romanian Orthodox Church in Nuremberg on the southern wall above the altar: Moses is

---

[18] Cf. Hans-Martin Barth: Die Theologie Martin Luthers. Eine kritische Würdigung, Gütersloh 2009, p. 193-229.
[19] See: Hans-Peter Grosshans: Geheimnis des Glaubens. Zum Thema der Theologie, ZThK 108, 2011, p. 472-489.

stepping near the bush. He has his shoes in his hands. And in the bush, there are burning leaves – and Mary with Christ in their midst.[20]

(detail)

From Saint Petersburg I show you a photograph of a mosaic in the cathedral "Saviour on the Blood". You find it not far from the entrance on the northern side on one pillar:

(The photo was taken on March 1st, 2018.)

From this painting tradition we learn: Christian theologians have reflected about the question, what person was meant, who is revealing himself? And they have

---

[20] Grigore und Maria Popescu (Ed.): op. cit. (like note: 4), picture on p. 24 and 230. In this church only Christ was painted as a picture for God!

answered: Only that person, who is the revelation of God for us: Christ. The bush is burning because God is within it. But it will not be consumed. It is able to bear the presence of God. And now these theologians have understood in a meditative way that also Mary was in that danger, because she had God within herself. But she also was not consumed.

One quote I can give you – from the 4th century theologian Gregorius of Nyssa: "Like there in the bush the fire was burning but it did not consume the bush, so here in the virgin the light was born – but without the loss of virginity."[21]

I would not restrict this experience only to Mary. I think: In a similar way this experience also belongs to us: We are not consumed. We can withstand this presence. We experience the side of love to us. And this side of love we can trust in!

4.2. I want to draw your attention to an initiative of our time which is meant without any religious aspect but which has – I think – deep religious dimensions: the collection of forgiveness stories by Marina Cantacuzino and Brian Moody[22]:

The murderer said: "Silvester 1997 a friend made a party. We took drugs and were heavily drinking. Conflicts arose and disturbing noise. A man came up the staircase and said that we should go. But my friend hit him that he fell down, and I was stepping against his head for four times. Then I went to the next party, without knowing that I had made the heaviest mistake of my life."
The widow explained: "Half an hour after Bob was killed, I was standing next to his dead body in the clinic. Then I went home to tell my four years old twins Emma and Sam that their daddy is dead. In the town there was a law of silence. No one called the police. No one told the truth. The fact that Bob was killed was terrible. But the silence was even more terrible. I had to move somewhere else."
The murderer: "The mystery of my crime started to destroy me. Maybe I would have to kill me, or instead: I had to end my silence."
The widow: "Four years later Ryan was arrested. The police showed him the video in which I was begging that he declares is guilt. He said: »I have done it«, and all the years of mourning and fear were ended. This sentence provoked a process of healing. Ryan asked the police to meet me! One day after his arresting I stood in front of that man who had murdered my husband."

---

[21] For this quote see: H. and M. Schmidt: Die vergessene Bildersprache christlicher Kunst. Ein Führer zum Verständnis der Tier-, Engel- und Mariensymbolik, München ²2018, p. 231.
[22] Cf. Bernhard Borgeest: Die Macht der Vergebung, FOCUS 12/2009, p. 78-83.

The murderer: "I wanted to excuse me – from face to face. But for Katy's forgiveness I never was prepared!"[23]

The reporter of this "forgiveness project" writes: "Those who are finally able to forgive are telling about a kind of redemption, of a kind of liberation out of the jail of suffering, of a kind of inner peace, sometimes of a kind of triumph about the murderer, but never of a kind of feeling of weakness. »Only who is strong can forgive« – Mahatma Gandhi has said."[24]

4.3. This idea is important for me: Who forgives is doing something good for the person who has become guilty but also – and even more – for himself or herself! This deep insight we also have into our biblical tradition – on important places within the Old Testament and within the New Testament:

«[…]но люби ближнего твоего, как самого себя, Я Господь» (Левит / Leviticus 19:18б/b).	"[…] but you shall love your neighbour as yourself: I am the Lord"
«Иисус отвечал ему: первая из всех заповедей: "слушай, Израиль! Господь Бог наш есть Господь единый; И возлюби Господа Бога твоего […]" […] Вторая подобная ей: "возлюби ближнего твоего, как самого себя"» (Марк / Mark 12:29.30a.31a).	"Jesus answered, »The first is, Hear, o Israel: The Lord our God, the Lord is one; and you shall love the Lord your God […]« […] The second is this, »You shall love your neighbour as yourself«"

The famous roman-catholic New Testament scholar Heinz Schürmann, who has taught many theologians and priests in the German Democratic Republic and whom I could have met explains: "The concentration of the whole law to these two commandments and their identification – that is really Jesus own work, for what there is no example before him."[25]

---

[23] Op. cit. (like note: 22), p. 79 (translation by myself).
[24] Op. cit. (like note 22), p. 83 (translation by myself).
[25] Heinz Schürmann: Worte des Herrn. Jesu Botschaft vom Königtum Gottes, Leipzig ⁵1994, p. 239 (translation by myself).

Additional we have to see that Jesus has positively taken up the presupposition of the Old Testament for loving the neighbour: Loving him or her like we love ourselves! It's not necessary to love others more than we love ourselves. To love another person like I love myself – that's the greatest thing what is possible.

These modern forgiveness stories are really important: They show that those who have forgiven another person, first have helped himself or herself! They have done something positive to oneself. They have gained liberation. One person in this forgiveness project had written: "It was a relief, not for him [the murderer of the daughter] but for myself."[26] This means: When we are able to do this good for us and forgive another person – then we renew our world for this person and for ourselves!

4.4. But now we have to do not only a next step but a step into a new quality, into a new dimension: So far Jesus Christ had become an example for us. And we feel ourselves on a way behind him, following him.

This first quality is like the modern practices on Facebook or on Instagram and so on: Many, many people are followers of their idols, followers of a star in television, of a star in the film culture, of a star in fashion, of a star in lifestyle and so on. And these idols have become so called trendsetters for their followers. This modern way of life is on vogue now! – But Jesus Christ is more than a trendsetter, more than a person with hundreds or thousands of followers.

Martin Luther had explained this "more" in June 1522 in a sermon on Matthew 16:13-19, on the confession of Peter: "Our natural understanding only can grasp Christ as a holy and pious man, who had given a wonderful example, we now have to follow. [...] But, who understands him in this way, only as example of a good life, to him or her the heaven still is closed and he or she has not yet understood Christ in an appropriate way. [...] The different and correct understanding of Christ is the following one [...]: »... not one who is going forward. But it is much higher with you: you are the Christ, the holy son of God«."[27]

This is the main and most important challenge of our faith: Are we ready to identify that side of God which is in favor of us in Jesus Christ? Are we ready to seeing the only possibility to encounter with God in Jesus Christ? Are we ready to show

---

[26] Op. cit. (like note 22), p. 81 (translation by myself).
[27] Martin Luther: Sermon von der Gewalt Sankt Peters, 29. Juni 1522, WA 10, III, p. 208ff. Cf. also my small study: Martin Luther für uns heute, Erlangen 2008, p. 13 (translation by myself).

others who are asking us for God this Jesus Christ as the only way to God? That this is important Luther had already shown by turning into a new way of speaking: He is not explaining any more but he is proclaiming and addressing: "But it is much higher with <u>you</u>: <u>you</u> are the Christ"!

Three years before his sermon on the confession of Peter Martin Luther had written to Georg Spalatin, the private secretary of the Elector Frederic the Wise: "God does not want that we come on another way to him, that we acknowledge him on another way, that we love him on another way, because he said (John 14:6): «Я есмь путь и истина и жизнь; никто не приходит к Отцу как только чрез Меня» / »I am the way, and the truth, and the life; no one comes to the Father, but by me«. May you listen: It is the deep conviction that nobody can come to the father except through Christ. In this way train yourself [...]."²⁸

4.5.1. May I now explain this deep insight on a special way: I want to ask how we may paint a picture of God. And I invite you to open yourself to this question really in an open way.

On April 3ʳᵈ, 2017, I visited the museum of the town Samara in Russia and have found there in the collection of ikons an ikon on the Trinity – not painted in the traditional orthodox way (which is a quotation of Genesis 18:1-15 of the visit of the three men by Abraham) but painted as an old man, as a younger man and as a dove.

And I recognized: The younger man, Jesus Christ, has the gloriole with the cross and the three letters: "O ΩN", through what he is marked as the picture of God. But next to him, this old man, also has a gloriole and above this gloriole there is written: «Господь Саваоф»²⁹ / "the Lord of hosts" – the word about God in Исаия / Isaiah 6:3. And this shows the problem to me: These two terms and pictures for the one God are painted and explained together! I think we <u>should not</u> do this. Otherwise we would give arguments to the Muslims who blame us that we would add something to God, that we would honor more

---

²⁸ Martin Luther: Brief an Georg Spalatin vom 12. February 1519, WA Br 1, p. 329 (translation by myself).
²⁹ Exactly: «ГДЬ САУАΩΦ», may be in Russian and Greek letters.

than one God. But we don't do this. We believe in <u>one</u> God! This one God has three shapes, has three ways to experience him – but only one picture: Christ! This we never should forget. I'm deeply convinced that we have to become again real Christians and withdraw all pictures of God as an old man: <u>Christ is the only picture of God.</u>

4.5.2. There is a first problem: We do not have an authentic picture of Jesus Christ. But we have a very convincing tradition of how to paint Jesus Christ. Maybe this tradition is connected with a picture of Jesus Christ on old shrouds,[30] maybe this tradition has other roots – but what is clear is the fact that there is a tradition how to paint Jesus in which we normally acknowledge whether a painted person should show Jesus or not. I suggest that we can follow this tradition.

And there is a second problem: This picture of Jesus is characterized in a way that we understand: This is a picture of God. Better: This is <u>the</u> picture of God. To paint it in this way makes us to Christians. The artists have done it in the following way: They have painted a gloriole with a cross and on the three parts of the cross three letters: on the above part an omicron – "O", on the left part an omega – "Ω" and on the right part a ny – "N".

One important example you all know is the "not with human hand painted picture", the „αχειροποιητον εικων", the «нерукотворный образъ».[31]

I present to you a special small ikon I had bought on July 16th 2014 in Ordino (Andorra).[32] Especially fascinating for me was the fact that the face of Christ of this ikon looks a little bit like it would have been painted by the famous artist Николай Константинович Рёрих / Nikolaj Konstantinowitsch Roerich.[33] Through Christ "the Being" is

---

[30] Cf. Ian Wilson: Jesus. The Evidence, New York 1988, and: Werner Bulst and Heinrich Pfeiffer: Das Turiner Grabtuch und das Christusbild, Band II: Das echte Christusbild, Frankfurt am Main 1991.
[31] See: Karl-Christian Felmy: Das Buch der Christus-Ikonen, Freiburg, Basel, Wien 2004, p. 20-25.
[32] The ikon is 10,5 cm x 13,5 cm; on her backpage is written «Икона сувенирная» "Souvenir-Ikon", what I understand in the way that this ikon was not consecrated. The artist is «Л.В. Лохна», the firm is «ЛИГАТУРА ЛТД» in Kiew.
[33] Vgl.: Пермский Иконостас Николая Рериха, Самара 2003 / Permer Ikonostas of Nikolaj Roerich, Samara 2003, for example on p. 71 the picture of an ikone "Not with human hand painted picture" from 1907. And: Е.П. Маточкин: Образ Иисуса Христа, Самара 2007 / E.P. Matotschkin:

looking to us, is looking to us the power, which will be new again and again, is looking to us God himself!

What's the source these letters are coming from? We have understood already that the Jewish translators of Exodus 3:14 who translated it into the Greek language have translated the Hebrew אֶהְיֶה אֲשֶׁר אֶהְיֶה with the Greek "Ο ΩΝ"![34] We have been wondering how the Christian theologians have identified within the burning bush a picture of Mary and Jesus Christ. Now we recognize this important second step: That one who is revealing himself as "the Being" for Christians only can be Jesus Christ!

Picture of Jesus Christ, Samara 2007, from the Серия «Николай Рерих: Вестник Красоты» / the series „Nikolaj Roerich: Bote der Schönheit", p. 44. There is documented the picture „Erlösers über der Tür" / "Redeemer above the door" in the church in Pskow of 1913.

[34] See above: 2.1. and 3.1.

God offers Peace – a more than 2.600 Years old Conviction of Faith,
Text: Числа / Numbers 6:22-27,
June 7th, 2020, and March 15th, 2022.[35]

«Благодать Господа нашего Иисуса Христа, и любовь Бога Отца, и общение Святого Духа со свеми вами. Аминь.»

"The grace of our Lord Jesus Christ, the love of God and the fellowship of the Holy Spirit be with you all. Amen."

Дорогие Сёстры и Братья! Dear Sisters and Brothers!

Because we all know it well, I first want to read the Biblical word for our sermon:

«И сказал Господь Моисею, говоря:
Скажи Аарону и сынам его:
Так благословляйте сынов Израилевых, говоря им:
Да благословит тебя Господь и сохранит тебя!
Да призрит на тебя Господь светлым лицем Своим и помилует тебя!
Да обратит Господь лице Своё на тебя и даст тебе мир!
Так пусть призывают имя Моё на сынов Израилевых,
и Я благословлю их»
(Числа / Numbers 6:22-27).

"The Lord said to Moses:
Say to Aaron and his sons:
Thus you shall bless the people of Israel: you shall say to them,
The Lord bless you and keep you:
The Lord make his face to shine upon you, and be gracious to you:
The Lord lift up his countenance upon you, and give you peace.
So they shall put my name upon the people of Israel,
and I will bless them"

Years ago, I have visited the Israel Museum in Jerusalem. Never I forget that I could go into one room and see there the vitrine with the two silver sheets which originally were moved to scrolls – sheets which had rolled up by the archeologists during a period of three years. And then on each of them a nearly similar word of blessing was found:

---

[35] This sermon was originally written for the homepage of "Göttinger Predigten im Internet".

«Да благословит тебя Господь и сохранит тебя! Да призрит на тебя Господь светлым лицем Своим и даст тебе мир!»	"The Lord bless you and keep you: The Lord make his face to shine upon you, and give you peace!"[36]

As I was standing in front of the vitrine also two nuns had come and looked what would be of interest. There I said to them: "Even today we're blessing with these sentences." – Because I knew in our Roman-Catholic Sister-Church only blessings like this:

«Да благословит тебя всемогущий Бог – Отец, Сын и Святый Дух!»	"The gracious God bless you – the Father, the Son and the Holy Spirit!"

And I told them that I knew the blessing from the book of Числа / Numbers from my Lutheran Church. The two sisters were very deeply impressed.

The discovery of these two silvern scrolls we have to understand better, because this discovery puts this blessing into a lively context: The excavator Gabrial Barkay worked from 1975 to 1983 in the cemetery of Ketef Hinnom, southwest of the City of David of Jerusalem near the church of St. Andrews.[37] The old graves had been cut into the rock. Because later the upper part was cut off many graves now are open and empty. But beneath of one grave Barkay found an artificial cave for the bones of the dead and the things which had been given to them – untouched! The bones of approximately 100 persons have been found, and many things: potteries, jewels. One interesting truth had been discovered: In that tomb a rich family from Jerusalem had put their dead persons from the 7th century before Christ until the 5th century before Christ and then also in the 1st century before Christ – this means: over the time of Babylonian Conquest of Jerusalem in the years 597 before Christ and 587/86 before Christ and also over the time of the Babylonian Exile![38] This family and other wealth families have existed in Jerusalem during all of these times! And together with the discovered jewels also our silvern scrolls from the end of the 7th century before Christ, may be from the year

---

[36] Cf. Emmanuel Tov: Textual Criticism of the Hebrew Bible, Minneapolis, Assen/Maastricht 1992, p. 379. There the reconstruction of the text is given in Hebrew.
[37] Cf. Dan Bahat: The illustrated Atlas of Jerusalem, New York and Jerusalem 1990, p. 18-19. And: Amihai Mazar: Archaeology of the Land of the Bible. 10,000 – 586 B.C.E., New York, London and so on, 1992, p. 522.
[38] Cf. Amihai Mazar, op. cit. (note 37), p. 516-517.521-526. And: Hershel Shanks: Jerusalem. An Archaeological Biography, New York 1995, p. 115-119.

610 before Christ, have been found[39] – or according to a new reconstruction: From the time between 507 to 495 before Christ.[40]

How I do imagine this? Two dead – may be a husband and his wife –, had worn around their necks these silvern amulets during their live time.[41] So they have lived with this prayer:

«Да благословит тебя Господь	"The Lord bless you
и сохранит тебя!	and keep you:
Да призрит на тебя Господь	The Lord make his face
светлым лицем Своим	to shine upon you,
и даст тебе мир!»	and give you peace!"

As they had become dead, these amulets were kept around their necks. – But silver is precious. Why would they have not been taken? And as the bones were collected in the bones cave one year later even then these amulets also were given into this cave! Because especially in the "existence" in the grave, in being assembled with the fathers and mothers, it was important that God would make his face shine upon him and her:

«Да призрит на тебя Господь	"The Lord make his face
светлым лицем Своим	to shine upon you,
и даст тебе мир!»	and give you peace!"

Isn't this a hope of peace which may strengthen also us even 2.632 or 2.522 years later?!

Counted from the first reconstructed date, we could say: Maybe 60 years later, in the exile in Babylonia, theologians have written texts about the identity of their people from Juda. And they have used this blessing in a longer version:

«Да благословит тебя Господь	"The Lord bless you
и сохранит тебя!	and keep you:
Да призрит на тебя Господь	The Lord make his face
светлым лицем Своим	to shine upon you,
и помилует тебя!	and be gracious to you:
Да обратит Господь лице Своё на тебя	The Lord lift up his countenance upon you,
и даст тебе мир!»	and give you peace."

---

[39] Cf. Emmanuel Tov, op. cit. (note 36), p. 118.
[40] Cf. Angelika Berlejung: Ein Programm fürs Leben. Theologisches Wort und anthropologischer Ort der Silberamulette von Ketef Hinnom, ZAW / Zeitschrift für Alttestamentliche Wissenschaft 120, 2008, p. 204-230, especially: p. 211-212.
[41] From Angelika Berlejung I learned that on the scrolls are also names mentioned. But she does not report these names (op. cit. [note 40], p. 212).

Through these amulets from the cemetery southwest of Jerusalem we have realized, that this word really addresses each single person: I can feel that I'm personally addressed:

«Да благословит <u>тебя</u>…,	"The Lord bless you…,
«Да призрит на <u>тебя</u>…,	"The Lord make his face to shine…,
«Да обратит Господь лице Своё на <u>тебя</u>…».	"The Lord lift up his countenance upon you…"

But the way how this blessing is organized in the book of Числа / Numbers shows us that it has in mind the whole community of the believers. Therefore, many pastors say this blessing in a plural formulation:

«Да благословит <u>вас</u> Господь и сохранит <u>вас</u>! Да призрит на <u>вас</u> Господь светлым лицем Своим и помылует <u>вас</u>! Да обратит Господь лице Своё на <u>вас</u> и даст <u>вам</u> мир!»	"The Lord bless you and keep you: The Lord make his face to shine upon you, and be gracious to you: The Lord lift up his countenance upon you, and give you peace."[42]

But I have to confess, that I like more the formulation in singular! When each single person is addressed then also the community of all these single persons is really blessed.

And this quotation of the old blessing in the book of Числа / Numbers presents to us a special challenge: To say the blessing is bound to «Аарону и сынам его» / "Aaron and his sons", is bound to the priests. Are only the priests allowed to bless? Maybe you have one time seen consciously in a Jewish cemetery the stones for dead men from families like Kohn and Katz: On them often are shown two hands in the gesture of blessing. This shows until now this special duty. As I know near the end of a worship service in a synagogue the present person from such a family is asked to bless the community. I can realize this only with acknowledgment and honor.

But for us as Christians is important, that we have made a different decision: Martin Luther had written in the year of 1520: "What has come out of baptism, may

---

[42] In English with the identical "you"!

be proud that it is already blessed to being priest […]."[43] Each baptized Christian may be ready to bless persons he or she knows: friends, family members, his and her grandparents, his and her parents, the own children! This Bible word for the sermon encourages us to this wonderful, to this blessed possibility: Really doing blessing by putting the hands on the head of another person! As I had started my service in my congregation in Altenburg in the fall of the year 1985, I had to lead the worship service for children who started the time in school. And during that worship service I have blessed all children, who stood in half of a circle, with my raised hands. After the worship service my colleague asked me a question I never forget: "What was this for a sparse blessing you have given?" To each girl, to each boy I should have gone and had put my hands on her and his head and give the blessing personally. When I'm now in the situation to bless a smaller group, I would bless all in this way, and I would look that I never will give such a sparse blessing again!

Now we have to think about this Bible word on the Sunday of Trinity. I imagine that the three parts of the old blessing had led to the connection with our Christian conviction. I will try it in the following way:

«Да благословит тебя Господь и сохранит тебя!» – Бог, Отец / "The Lord bless you and keep you!" – God, the Father,
«Да призрит на тебя Господь светлым лицем Своим и помилует тебя!» – Бог, Сын / "The Lord make his face to shine upon you, and be gracious to you!" – God, the Son,
«Да обратит Господь лице Своё на тебя и даст тебе мир!» – Бог, Святый Дух / "The Lord lift up his countenance upon you, and give you peace." – God, the Holy Spirit.

This deepens our faith in the One God as Father, Son and Holy Spirit: God, the Father, blesses us and keeps us. God, the Son, makes his face to shine upon us. God, the Holy Spirit, lifts up his countenance upon us and gives us peace. This is like a special revelation about this difficult and often unclear knowledge of "Trinity". To this festivity today this special offer is given to us. May we take it!

Then I have found a hymn in our German hymn book, which takes up all our insights in a special way. In the year 1978 in the community of Gnadenthal in Northern Bavaria a hymn about Числа / Numbers 6 was produced which enables us to sing together this word of blessings:

---

[43] Martin Luther: An den christlichen Adel deutscher Nation von des christlichen Standes Besserung, 1520. The English translation is by myself.

"Bless us, o Lord! Your face may shine upon us and be gracious – eternally.
Bless us, o Lord! Put your angels around us! Keep us in your peace – eternally."[44]

This hymn only becomes a threefold hymn by repeating the first stance after the second one. And this is suggested – as part of the poetry. And this offers a special kind of meditation. But: When you are singing or reading only these stances 1 and 2, then you are coming near to the prayer of the two silver scrolls from Ketef Hinnom – what the authors in Gnadenthal never could have known! I want to put these both texts next to each other:

2632 or 2.522 years old:	44 years old:
»Да благословит тебя Господь и сохранит тебя! Да призрит на тебя Господь светлым лицом Своим	"Bless us, o Lord! Your face may shine upon us and be gracious – eternally. Bless us, o Lord! Put your angels around us! Keep us in your peace – eternally."
и даст тебе мир!«	

Дорогие Сёстры и Братья! / Dear Sisters and Brothers! Have you ever seen the similar conviction of faith, the similar hope of faith so deeply convincing – over approximately 2.600 years? I'm convinced: We can stay to this hope of faith, to this conviction of faith with inner strength! That's the offering of the Sunday of today. May we take it!
Amen.

| «И мир Божий, который превыше всякого ума, соблюдёт сердца ваши и помышления ваши во Христе Иисусе!» | "And the peace of God which passes all understanding, will keep your hearts and your minds in Christ Jesus." |

---

[44] Cf. Evangelisches Gesangbuch, Nr. 573. The English translation is by myself. The original German text is as follows:
„Segne uns, o Herr! Laß leuchten dein Angesicht über uns und sei uns gnädig ewiglich. Segne uns, o Herr! Deine Engel stell um uns! Bewahre uns in deinem Frieden ewiglich!"

"God has made everything beautiful", Qohälät / Проповедник / Ecclesiastes 3:11[45]

Дорогие Сёстры и Братья! Dear Sisters and Brothers!

In the second century before Christ in Jerusalem existed a kind of private think tank. This was a private school of discussion, in which the members have reflected about basic problems of human life and about the relation to God. An important person within this think tank was the one who gave inputs into the discussion, and who has summarized the results and explained them. We can call him the "Speaker of the Gathering". This means he was the one, who brought together what was discussed and what was learned.

In Hebrew a term for gathering, for meeting together is »קהל« – "qāhāl". Therefore, this person was called »קהלת« – "qohälät", which often is translated with «проповедник» – "preacher".

But I think, this term does create too much the picture of a person who always stands in front of a congregation and talks to it. Instead, this wise man took up what the other members of the think tank have argued and gives words for it. Therefore, I think "Speaker of the Gathering" is more precise.

What was discussed in that private school later was put together and written down and transferred to the temple. Therefore, finally it was integrated into the collection of holy literature. But even in the second century after Christ serious discussions were going on, whether this book really can be understood as a part of the holy literature. Finally, the groups who wanted this succeeded – and we have now the book of "Qohälät" within the Hebrew Bible of our Jewish friends and also within our Christian Old Testament.

It's very interesting to read sometimes in this book. I invite you to do this. In Russian: «Книга Екклесиаста или Проповедника» – "Book Ecclesiastes or The Preacher". This year the church has decided to take one sentence of this book as the biblical word for the month September. It is a conclusion of the discussion

---

[45] This meditation I had given in the worship service on Sunday, September 2nd, 2018, in the Congregation in Tscheboksary, at the Wolga, of the Evangelical Lutheran Church of Ingria in the Russian Federation.

about the meaning and the role of time in our life within chapter 3 of the book "Speaker of the Gathering". This sentence sounds:

«Все соделал Он [Бог]	"He [God] has made everything
прекрасным в своё время,	beautiful in its time;
и вложил мир	also he has put eternity
в сердце их,	into man's mind,
хотя человек хотя может	yet so that he cannot find out
постигнуть дел,	
который Бог делает,	what God has done
от начало до конца»	from the beginning to the end"
(Проповедник / Ecclesiastes 3:11).	

Do you understand your life? Do I understand my life? Sometimes I look back and remember what had happened in the different phases of my life. Sometimes I can identify factors which have influenced developments and decisions. But often I feel that this touches the surface only. And why it happened and what was the deeper meaning or what still is the deeper meaning I do not know really. I suppose you will agree for your life: «мы не можем постигнуть дел» – "we cannot find out what happens" in our life. That's the first step.

And now this group of wise Jewish men in Jerusalem gave a first answer. That's the second step. They said: «который Бог делает» – "what God has done". It is not normal to think of a God and to argue that this God is active within our lives. This is really the first answer: There is a God. And this God shapes our life. To be a Christian means: To open oneself to this belief. to this conviction: Yes, I understand nothing, but I keep to this conviction that God is, and that God acts in my life.

Now we have the third step before us: Because God is the actor, we can say: «Все соделал Он [Бог] прекрасным в своё время!» – "He [God] has made everything beautiful in its time!» I'm deeply convinced that there is no possibility to come to this conclusion by arguing. To reflect, to exchange the pros and cons and then realize: «Все соделал Бог прекрасным!» – "God has made everything beautiful!" No. This we can only believe. That's the result of our faith. Already against many experiences, and also because of some different experiences we are invited to proclaim: «Все соделал Бог прекрасным!» – "God has made everything beautiful!"

This is a sentence with hard discussion in its background. This is a sentence a "Qohälät", a «проповедник», a "Speaker of the Gathering" has formulated. Please, allow that I'm now your "Speaker of the Gathering", and that I may proclaim also in your name: «Все соделал Бог прекрасным!» – "God has made everything beautiful!"

Аминь – Amen.

Do exist Messianic Texts in our Old Testament? Prepared for: Чебоксары, Russia, 2021[46]

Dedicated to the 55th birthday of my former student, Prof. Dr. Tonio Sebastian Richter, Leipzig and Berlin, on January 14th, 2022.

1.

We call ourselves and we are called by others as the "Christians". What does this mean?

1.1. In a modern German translation of the Koran at all places where this conviction is given the translators, Prof. Dr. Hartmut Bobzin and his spouse Katharina Bobzin, have translated with "Christ" or "Christians".[47] To this wonderful translation I only have in connection with these terms the question: Does really the Koran is speaking about Jesus as the "Christ" and about us as the "Christians"? Four years ago, I have expressed my doubts whether it is the best solution using these terms.[48] There I had said that the terms "Christ" and "Christians" could be understood in the way that the Koran would accept these identifications: Yes, he was the "Christ"; yes, they are the "Christians". Would our Moslem friends accept this? Because of that I follow at these places an older translation which I had bought during my study time in the German Democratic Republic.[49] This translation used for the term "'al masich" "the Messiah" for Jesus and for the term "Naṣārā" "the Nazarenes" for us the Christians. These terms do say in the German language only what is written in the Arabic language.

1.2. The Hebrew language has for an "Anointed One" only the term "מָשִׁיחַ" / "Maschiach" – "Messiah" and the New Testament only has the term "Χριστος" – "Christ", even when it wants to speak about other persons than Jesus, whom it calls the "Christ". May I remind you: We all know that in history many persons have been called and identified as "Messiahs", because they have been identified

---

[46] This paper was prepared for a visit in congregations in Russia what was not possible because of the Covid Pandemie. I'm not sure whether it will be possible in 2022, because still there is the war against Ukraine.

[47] Der Koran. Aus dem Arabischen neu übertragen von Hartmut Bobzin unter Mitarbeit von Katharina Bobzin, München ²2015.

[48] Rainer Stahl: Martin Luther inspiriert und regt zum Widerspruch an. Teil 2, in: Религия. Церковь. Общество, Выпуск VII, Санкт-Петербург 2018, p.56-58.

[49] Der Koran. Übersetzung von Max Henning, Leipzig 1970.

with this hope of a Messianic person. See only the sentence in the Gospel of Matthew 24:23:

"Τότε εάν τις υμιν ειπη ιδου ο χριστος, η ωδε, μη πιστεύσητε!" /
„Wenn dann jemand zu euch sagen wird: Siehe, hier ist der Christus!, oder: Da!, so sollt ihr's nicht glauben." /
"Then if any one says to you, »Lo, here is the Christ!« or »There he is!« do not believe it." /
«Тогда, если кто скажет вам: "вот здесь Христос", или "там", – не верьте».

This means: In the past there have been persons identified as "Messiahs". And when we as Christians identify Jesus of Nazareth as "the Messiah", as "the Christ", then we realize the fundamental identification from our side: We have decided that all discussions about questions of the identification have come to an end and only one would be possible: This Jesus of Nazareth is the "Messiah", is the "Christ".

And this means: All persons who identify this Jesus of Nazareth as the "Christ" are showing that by this identification they are "Christians". If we would not do this we could not be called as "Christians". This we never should forget! Especially because of the inaccuracy of our time: Many people speak about Jesus Christ without the conviction that he the "Christ", the "Messiah" is. They could not speak about Jesus Christ but should always say Jesus of Nazareth!

2.

2.1. First of all, I want to explain the way to give the dates in history. May I explain this not only from theoretical facts but from an experience: In fall of 2016 I have bought in the archeological park of the "City of David" in Jerusalem the book "Excavating the City of David. Where Jerusalem's History began" by Ronny Reich. The author always writes of a certain year BCE or of a certain year CE. These short forms mean "Before the Common Era / Before the Current Era / Before the Christian Era" or "the Common Era / the Current Era / the Christian Era".[50] I suppose that the Jewish archaeologist Ronny Reich from Israel means always "Current Era" or "Common Era" and "Before the Common Era" or "Before the Current Era". Only convinced Christian persons will understand this form in the way: "the Christian Era" and "Before the Christian Era".

---

[50] I give only one example by Ronny Reich: Excavating the City of David. Where Jerusalem's History began, Jerusalem 2011, p.: 325: „The last part of the Second Temple period, sometimes called the Herodian period, extends over the second half of the first century BCE and the first century CE, until 70 CE."

Jesus of Nazareth was may be born in the year 5 "Before the Common Era" or like we Christians would say: in the year 5 "Before the Christian Era". And he was murdered in the year 30 of the "Common Era" or of the "Christian Era". Already the second possibility of counting shows a fundamental decision, we cannot expect by persons and cultures which are not influenced by Christianity. But additionally, I mention that since 2021 a publication exists in which the year of the birth of Jesus concerning Luke 2:2 is identified in the time of the governor of Syria, Quirinius, in December 6 CE or January 7 CE and his crucifixion to April 23rd, 34 CE.[51] This position has to be discussed.

Additionally, I may report an experience of my life: In my school years in the German Democratic Republic in history no one was speaking about "Before the Christian Era" or about the "Christian Era". In those days always was said: "Before our time" or "Of our time"!

May I add another observation which I made by reading the book "Masada" by Jodi Magness:[52] There the dates in the past are given by "before Christ" or by "after Christ". When she gives such an information within a sentence she writes: „[…] innerhalb des im fünften nachchristlichen Jahrhundert gebauten […]"[53] / "within the fifth post-Christian century" or „[…] von Mikwen aus dem ersten vorchristlichen und ersten nachchristlichen Jahrhundert […]"[54] / "of Mikwaoth from the first pre-Christian and from the first post-Christian century". Because I do not know what the Israelian author had written in English, I only can underline: The German translation identifies the "Common Era" / the "Christian Era" as "post-Christian time" and makes a statement which goes beyond a simple information about a time! I'm convinced that we never should speak about the time after the earthly lifetime of Jesus of Nazareth like it would be a time after Christianity because we Christians are still active.

2.2. Now we have to understand that the time in which Jesus of Nazareth was living was a time in which many persons and groups within Judaism did expect a "Messiah". This was the time in which many texts of the tradition were understood in a new way: as texts of the hope for a "Messiah". When we will read some

---

[51] See Uwe Jochum: In der Mitte der Zeit. Die neue Chronologie des Lebens Jesu, Hildesheim, Zürich, New York 2021, p. 64-68 and p. 103.
[52] Jodi Magness: Masada. Der Kampf der Juden gegen Rom, Wissenschaftliche Buchgesellschaft, Darmstadt 2020. The English Original – "Masada. From Jewish Revolt to Modern Myth" – was published in 2018 in Princeton.
[53] Jodi Magness, op. cit., p. 151.
[54] Jodi Magness, op. cit., p. 280.

texts (see part 3) we always have to prove as far as they could understood as texts about a "Messiah" and what this did mean and does mean until today!

When persons wanted to identify a person as a "Messiah" they had to understand several texts of their religious tradition as texts which would speak about a "Messiah", like they would speak about a "Messiah". This new understanding for the group of the "Christians" is expressed in the New Testament in two ways:

First as the followers of the "way" – see Acts 24:14: "κατα »την οδον« ην λεγουσιν αιρεσιν" / „nach »dem Weg«, den sie eine Sekte nennen" / "that according to »the Way«, which they call a sect" / «что по "учению" [here should be written: "пути"], которое они называют ересью». And cf. Acts 9:2: "οπως εαν τινας ευρη »της οδου« οντας ανδρας τε και γυναικας…" / „dass er Anhänger »dieses Weges«, Männer und Frauen, wenn er sie fände…" / "so that if he found any belonging to the Way, men or women…" / «кого найдёт последующих сему "учению", и мужчин и женщин…» [again with "учение" = "Doctrin"].

Secondly as the "Christians", or how this term may be translated: as the "Messiah-People"[55] – see Acts 11:26c: "χρηματισαι τε πρωτως εν Αντιοχεια τους μαθητας »Χριστιανους«" / „In Antiochia wurden die Jünger zuerst »Christen« genannt" or, as I said: „In Antiochia wurden die Jünger zuerst »Messiasleute« genannt" / "and in Antioch the disciples were for the first time called »Christians«" or: "Messiah-People" / «в Антиохии в первый раз стали называться "Христианами"».

And: This term "Christians" became fundamental for the following decades and centuries until today. This understanding is the basis for the Christian understanding of these texts, for the understanding that these texts can be understood as texts which are speaking about Jesus of Nazareth, "the Christ".

2.3. A short additional note: In this period "before the Current Era" and in the beginning of "the Current Era" a ready and finalized "Old Testament" did not yet exist. To identify texts of the Jewish religious tradition as an "Old Testament" needs texts which were called "New Testament" and persons who are understanding themselves as "Christians". But in those years Christians did not yet exist –

---

[55] Cf. Michael Theobald: Kirche im Neuen Testament. Ein ekklesiologischer Entwurf in vierundzwanzig Thesen, ZThK 117, 2020, p. 377-408; there p. 379-380, note 7: „Die in Antiochien aufgekommene Rede von den Χριστιανοί, den »Messiasleuten« (Apg 11,26), unterscheidet aus einer Außenperspektive die *jüdischen* Jesus-Gläubigen von anderen *jüdischen* Gruppierungen hinsichtlich ihres messianischen Bekenntnisses."

and within the Jewish religious community even a "Bible" did not yet exist. Only later the diverse Jewish religious literature would be discussed and out of it a certain collection of books was put together as the "Bible". Jesus of Nazareth himself was talking about the "the law and the prophets" / «закон и пороки» (Матфея 7:12) and also about the "Psalms" / «Псалмы». These terms meant first collections of books and single books which later have become together the "Bible" – the "Hebrew Bible".

2.4. One detail I have to add: We have to see the Greek translation of the theological literature: From the 3rd century BCE on was the time in which the old texts have been translated into the Greek language, in which the collection of holy texts was built which we call "the Septuagint". About this translation I can give a general statement: Not the Hebrew version of these texts is that one, which expresses the expectation of a "Messiah", of a "Christ" as a figure of the final time – but their Greek translations, this means their forms in the Septuagint is it! This Jewish translation shows the new expectations within the Jewish community from the 3rd or 2nd century BCE on! This means: When we are looking for messianic texts in our Bible, we always have to compare such interpretations in the Greek language!

3.

May I now give you some rare examples:

3.1.

I want to start with a text which was found in cave 4 in Qumran, near the Dead Sea, a text maybe from the year 90 BCE. It's a small text in the document 4Q521, fragment 2, column II. This text is part of a messianic apocalypse, which we call "About the Resurrection". I read only some lines:

„[…] der Himmel und die Erde
werden hören auf seinen Gesalbten,
[…]
dann heilt Er Durchbohrte,
und Tote belebt Er,
Armen verkündet Er Gutes,
Verlassene wird Er leiten
und Hungernde reich machen […]."[56]

«[…] небо и земля
услышат Своего Помазанника,
[…]
Потом исцелит Он израненных,
и оживит мёртвых,
Облагодетельствует бедных,
Покинутым укажет путь,
И обогатит голодных […].»[57]

---

[56] Published in: Johann Maier: Die Qumran-Essener: Die Texte vom Toten Meer, Band II: Die Texte aus Höhle 4, UTB 1863, München, Basel 1995, p. 683-684. I'm not ready to imagine an English translation.

[57] The Russian translation of this text is by Ruth Stubenitzky, former translator in Nowosaratowka (2011). All other texts in this paper are Bible texts and quoted from your Russian Bible.

This text really shows us an eschatological hope, a hope of a person who will open the last, the final salvation for our world: The world will listen to "his Maschiach", to "his Messiah". And "his Messiah" will heal all who are in need, even will call the dead into new life!

What we have seen in a text from outside the Biblical tradition we will find also within the Biblical tradition – which is for us Christians the "Old Testament" and for our Jewish friends the "Bible" –. We will find it in the Biblical tradition only on the way of a new interpretation – on the way to understand them as messianic texts, what we can see in the Greek Translation of the Septuagint! This we never should forget!

3.2.

3.2.1. In the Biblical collection of the "Psalms" we have hymns which have been originally connected with the Judean Kingdom in Jerusalem. They show how the kings and their theologians and priests have underlined their power. In Psalm / Псалом 2 we found a quote of the ceremony of the inauguration of a new king:

Verses:

6a „»Ich aber habe meinen König eingesetzt
  b auf meinem heiligen Berg Zion.«
7a^1 Kundtun will ich den Ratschluss Jahwes.
  a^2 Er hat zu mir gesagt: »Du bist mein Sohn,
  b heute habe ich dich gezeugt.
8a^1 Bitte mich,
  a^2 so will ich dir Völker zum Erbe geben
  b und der Welt Enden zum Eigentum […].«"
	"»I have set my king
	on Zion, my holy hill.«
	I will tell of the decree of the Lord:
	He said to me: »You are my son,
	today I have begotten you.
	Ask of me,
	and I will make the nations your heritage,
	and the ends of the earth your possession […].«"

       6a «"Я помазал Царя Моего
         b над Сионом, святою горою Моею."
       7a^1 Возвещу определение:
         a^2 Господь сказал Мне: "Ты Сын Мой";
         b Я ныне родил Тебя;
       8a^1 Проси у Меня,
         a^2 и дам народы в наследие Тебе
         b и пределы земли во владение Тебе […].»
       (Psalm / Псалом 2:6-8).

Concerning verse 7 I can give you the solution of a slight difference: In the Hebrew original and in the German translation by Martin Luther the term "Jahve" / the "Lord" is given in the first quarter of this verse; this would be in Russian: «Возвещу Господь определение». And in the second quarter there is only the verb "to speak" in the third person singular but no "Jahve" / the "Lord". But your Russian translation has the term of «Господь» only in the second quarter of this verse: «Господь сказал Мне». Why is it? There you find in your translation partly the Greek translation of our psalm in the Septuagint: "διαγγέλλων τό πρόσταγμα κυρίου: Κύριος εἶπεν πρός με". There you find the term "Kyrios" in the first and in the second quarter of the verse. In Russian language would this be: «Возвещу Господь определение: Господь сказал Мне»! But you have only: «Возвещу определение: Господь сказал Мне». I think, this a wonderful example of the relation of your translation on the one hand to the Hebrew original and on the second hand to the Greek translation of the first half of the 2nd century BCE!

Compared with the Hebrew original from the time of the Judean kings this psalm was later also used in the time of weakness of the power of the kingdom and additionally in the time without any ruling king in Jerusalem. In those times this hope – «и дам народы в наследие Тебе / и пределы земли во владение Тебе» / "and I will make the nations your heritage, / and the ends of the earth your possession" – became the expectation of a final king, of a king of the last time after all history, of the eschatological king, of the "Messiah".

3.2.2. The nearly final text within the Book of Psalms, Psalm / Псалом 149, expresses the following hope:

Verses:

1a^1 „[…]
  a^2 „Singet dem Herrn ein neues Lied;
  b sein Lobpreis [sei] in der Versammlung
    der Frommen. […]
5a Es sollen jubeln die Frommen in
    Herrlichkeit […],
7a dass sie Rache üben unter den Völkern […],
9a dass sie an ihnen vollziehen das
    niedergeschriebene Gericht. […]"

"[…]
Sing to the Lord a new song,
his praise in the assembly of the faithful! […]
Let the faithful exult in glory […],
to wreak vengeance on the nations […],
to execute on them the judgment written!"

1a¹ «[…]
   a² Пойте Господу песнь новую;
   b   хвала Ему в собрании святых. […]
5a Да торжествуют святые во славе […].
7a Для того, чтобы совершать мщение
     над народами […].
9a Производить над ними
     суд писанный. […]»
(Psalm / Псалом 149:1,5a,7a,9a).

In the same way this psalm is expressed in the Septuagint. This shows that even the Hebrew original had spoken about a coming situation of the last time. And in the same way did it the translators of the 2nd century BCE into the Greek language! This means: The construction of the Psalter with the Psalms 2 and 49 as frame show that the whole Psalter should be understand in a messianic meaning: All hopes and images of a new life and world given by God have been understood as hopes and images of the coming final time, of the time of the "Messiah"!

3.3.

Now I want to draw your attention to a very important text you will know already: Isaiah / Исаия 7:14:

Vers:

14a „Darum gibt von selber mein Herr euch ein Zeichen.	"Therefore the Lord himself will give you a sign.
b¹ Da, die Junge wird schwanger und gebiert einen Sohn.	Behold, a young woman shall conceive and bear a son,
b² Seinen Namen soll sie rufen: Immanuel / Bei uns ist Gott!"	and shall call his name Immanu-el."

14a «Итак
    Сам Господь даст вам знамение:
  b¹ се, Дева во чреве приимет,
     и родит Сына,
  b² и нарекут имя Ему:
     Еммануил.»

My first step: We have to look at the German translation I had given: In this case I have not used the translation by Martin Luther – we will look at it later in our discussion of our text – but the important translation by the Jewish theologians Martin Buber and Franz Rosenzweig from the Twenties of the last century.[58] I have given it, because their German version is giving precisely the Hebrew text. And I have realized one very interesting detail: Each line in your Russian translation fits wonderfully to each line of the German translation by Buber and Rosenzweig. Therefore, we can use them and also the English translation to go into the questions and challenges of this very important verse of the Bible.

Now I have reflected about the question: How I could teach you all these aspects of this verse? For this I have used as basis what I had given 28 years ago in a paper in my old faculty in Jena, but published in Leipzig: „»Immanuel« – Gott mit uns?".[59] Today I cannot present all insights of this old paper to you. But some of them I want to explain to you. For this I have chosen the method to start with the last problem and then to go backwards:

3.3.1. The name of the announced son is in the Hebrew Bible „עִמָּנוּ אֵל" / "ʿimmānu El", is in the Septuagint "Εμμανουηλ", is in the translation by Martin Buber and Franz Rosenzweig „Immanuel", is in the English Bible "Immanuel", and is in your Russian Bible «Еммануил». They all are similar. And they say: "With us is God", like Martin Buber and Franz Rosenzweig had added: „Bei uns ist Gott!" This means: The original message of this story is, that God, that Jahve, will be at the side of the Judean king in Jerusalem, at the side of his dynasty – also in future. May I underline this for our understanding: This original message says not more but also not less.

3.3.2. Then we have to look carefully to the following question: Who will give the son his name? In the Hebrew text this question is clearly answered: the used verb has a feminine form. This means: The <u>woman</u>, the <u>mother</u> will give him his name. Therefore especially Martin Buber and Franz Rosenzweig had written: „seinen Namen soll <u>sie</u> rufen" / "his name <u>she</u> shall call", what is also said in the English translation. But in a manuscript from Qumran we also have a male form: "and he calls". And additionally in the Septuagint we have a form of a kind of addressing the king: "καὶ καλέσεις τό ὄνομα αυτου" / "and <u>you</u> will give him his name" – as I understand your Russian translation: «и нарекут имя Ему». Additionally the Gospel of Matthew quotes this word in plural: „καὶ καλέσουσιν τό

---

[58] Bücher der Kündung, Die Schrift 3, verdeutscht von Martin Buber gemeinsam mit Franz Rosenzweig, 8. Auflage der neubearbeiteten Ausgabe von 1958, Stuttgart 1992, p. 28.
[59] See: Rainer Stahl: „»Immanuel« – Gott mit uns?", in: Mitteilungen und Beiträge 8, Theologische Fakultät Leipzig, Forschungsstelle Judentum, 1994, p. 19-36.

ὄνομα αυτου" – "and someone [= God] will call his name" (cf. Matthew 1:23b). This means that you have the following possibilities:

+ First: As it was usual in old Juda: The mother has to decide the name of the son.

+ Or secondly: Here in his responsibility for the monarchy the king decides the name.

+ Or thirdly, what also could be possible: God himself will give him his name! Already a very unearthly understanding!

3.3.3. Now we come to the first challenge of our Bible quote: In Hebrew this verse 14 is speaking about a special young lady we could identify, if we would live in the 8th century "BCE" / "Before the Current Era" / "Before the Christian Era". In Hebrew it is connected with the article – „הַ" / "hā" –. This means: The following is said not about an unknown woman, but about a special one. Additionally, the term „עַלְמָה" / "ʿalmah" is used. This is the special term for a young lady who will become pregnant or is already pregnant and on her way to the first birth of a child.[60] So we can understand that this text originally was speaking about a famous wife from the harem of the king in Jerusalem. In that connection I have to give the additional information, that the term "virgin" in Hebrew sounds „בְּתוּלָה" / "bᵉtulah". And this term is <u>not</u> used in our story!

But why do you have here in your Russian translation the term «дева»? And even in our translation by Martin Luther we also have this term: „Siehe, eine Jungfrau ist schwanger [...]." Why they both can write about a "virgin" where within the Hebrew original this term is <u>not</u> used? Here again the Septuagint is important. The Jewish translators in the 2nd century BCE in Egypt have interpreted the Hebrew "ʿalmah" with the Greek word "παρθένος". And this really means „Jungfrau" / "virgin" / «дева».

3.3.4. Again, we have the result I already had expressed in part 2.4.: In the time in direction to the era of CE, of the "Common Era", of the "Christian Era" important theologians of the Jewish community have gone the step forward to an eschatological understanding! It is this interpretation in the Greek language which shows: The coming new person will open a really new situation and a new time and therefore will be able to bring the salvation for the whole world. Martin Rösel had written many years ago: The translators into the Greek language want to

---

[60] Here I underline that Martin Buber and Franz Rosenzweig have translated: "will become pregnant" / „wird schwanger".

express, „daß der kommende Heilsbringer von Beginn an dem normalen sündigen Lauf von Zeugung und Geburt enthoben ist, demnach einer neuen Zeit angehört und gerade deshalb die Möglichkeit zum Heil verbürgt" / "that the coming bringer of salvation is from the very beginning not part of the normal sinful way of procreation and birth, so that he is belonging to a new time and because of that he has the possibility to offer salvation".[61]

It this understanding what then leads to the identification of this basic text with Jesus of Nazareth – as it is shown in our Christian New Testament, especially given in Matthew 1:18-24 where his name "Jesus" is understood as the one who realizes God's plan to save the people. His name "Jesus", in Hebrew "J^{e}hoschu^{c}a", means: "Jahwe / the Lord is saving"! Therefore, in Matthew 1 an advice is given to Joseph:

„Und sie wird einen Sohn gebären, dem sollst du den Namen Jesus geben, denn er wird sein Volk retten von ihren Sünden" Sünden"	"She will bear a son, and you shall call his name Jesus, for he will save his people from their sins"

«Родит же Сына,
и наречешь Ему имя: Иисус;
ибо Он спасет людей Своих от грехов их»
(Matthäus / Matthew / Матфея 1:21).

These words give the answer to all questions about the meaning of this hope which has started may be around the year 100 BCE! And these words are formulated in an interesting parallelism to Isaiah 7:14![62]

3.3.5. In the beginning of the year 2020 in the newspaper of the Evangelical Church in Central Germany an interesting summary was published: Nicole Marten quoted in her article „Alles nur ein Missverständnis?" / "All only a misunderstanding?" a roman-catholic book about the problems of translation of the Bible and identified three equal possibilities of understanding of our passage:[63] „Im Falle der Jungfrau bedeutet dies: »Der hebräische Text von Jesaja spricht von

---

[61] Martin Rösel: Die Jungfrauengeburt des endzeitlichen Immanuel. Jesaja 7 in der Übersetzung der Septuaginta, Jahrbuch für Biblische Theologie (JBTH) 6, 1991, p. 135-151, quote: p. 150 (the translation into English is by myself).
[62] Finally, I can refer to a very important recent publication: Konrad Schmid and Jens Schröter: Die Entstehung der Bibel. Von den ersten Texten zu den heiligen Schriften, München ²2019, p. 297-298: They show that Justinus Martyr (+ 165) in his "Dialog with Trypho" explained that the Jewish translation of Isajah 7:14 into Greek is important for the correct understanding of this passage!
[63] „Glaube und Heimat", No. 3 of January 17th, 2020, p. 13.

einer jungen Frau und meint die junge gebärfähige Ehefrau des Königs; das Kind, das sie gebären wird, ist ein prophetisches Zeichen für eine bestimmte Zeitdauer, etwa sieben Jahre«. Die griechische Übersetzung des Jesaja-Textes machte daraus eine »Jungfrau«, die den Messias in der Zukunft gebären wird. Matthäus griff das auf und identifizierte die Jungfrau mit Maria, den Messias mit Marias Kind. »Man kann Jesaja 7,14 also mindestens auf zwei, vielleicht sogar auf drei Weisen lesen, und alles ist ‚richtig'«, sagt Thomas Hieke." / "In the case of the virgin it means: »The Hebrew Text in Isaiah speaks about a young lady and thinks of the young and pregnant woman of the king; the child, whom she will give birth is a prophetical sign for a certain period, approximately seven years«. The Greek translation of the Isaiah-text changes to a »virgin«, who will give birth to the Messiah of the future. Matthew took it and identified the virgin with Mary, and the Messiah with the child of Mary. »It is possible to read Isaiah 7:14 at least on two, may be even on three ways, and all are 'correct'«, says Thomas Hieke."[64] I'm convinced that it is really wonderful that these important insights, which I teach since decades, now are published in a newspaper for congregations!

3.4.

Finally, I would like to draw your attention to Daniel 7. This is a very important text because it's the basis of opinions which will be found even far beyond of the opinions which Daniel or following theologians under his name until 140 BCE had explained.

Verses:

13a	„Ich sah in diesem Gesicht in der Nacht,	"I saw in the night visions,
b¹	und siehe,	and behold,
b²	mit den Wolken des Himmels kam einer wie eines Menschen Sohn.	with the clouds oft he heaven came one like a son of man,
c	und bis zum Alten an Tagen gelangte er	and he came to the Ancient of Days
d	und vor ihn wurde er gebracht.	and was presented before him.
14a	Ihm wurde gegeben die Herrschaft und die Ehre und die Staatsgewalt[65].	And to him was given dominion and glory and kingdom,
b	Und alle Völker, Nationen und Sprachen – ihm werden sie dienen.	that all peoples, nations, and languages should serve him;
c	Seine Macht ist eine ewige Herrschaft,	his dominion is an everlasting dominion,

---

[64] Cf. Thomas Hieke and Konrad Huber (Ed.): Bibel falsch verstanden. Hartnäckige Fehldeutungen biblischer Texte erklärt, Stuttgart 2020 (translation into English by myself).
[65] In this connection I have the term „מַלְכוּ" / "malku" – "kingdom" consciously translated in a more general way with "state power".

		die nicht zerstört werden wird.	which shall not pass away,
	d	Und seine Staatsgewalt ist eine,	and his kingdom one
		die nicht zugrunde gehen wird.	that shall not be destroyed.
[…]			[…]
17a		Diese großen Tiere, derer vier sind,	These four great beasts are
	b	sind vier Staatsgewalten, die aus der	four kings who shall arise out of
		der Erden erstehen werden.	the earth.
18a		Aber die Staatsgewalt werden empfangen	But the saints of the Most High shall
		die Heiligen des Höchsten	receive the kingdom,
	b	und werden die Staatsgewalt besitzen	and possess the kingdom for ever,
		für Ewigkeiten und ewige Ewigkeiten"	for ever and ever"

13a   «Видел я в ночных видениях,
  b¹ вот,
  b² с облаками небесными шел
      как бы Сын человеческий,
  c   дошел до Ветхого днями
  d   и подведен был к Нему.
14a   И Ему дана власть, слава и царство,
  b   чтобы все народы, племна и языки
      служили Ему;
  c   владычество Его – владычество вечное,
      которое не прейдет,
  d   и царство Его не разрушится.
17a   Эти большие звери, которых четыре,
  b   что четыре царя восстанут от земли.
18a   Потом примут царство святые Всевышнего,
  b   и будут владеть царством вовек
      и во веки веков»
(Daniel 7:13a,14a.c,17,18).

3.4.1. I'm convinced that the original Aramaic text speaks about two fundamental different forms of power. On the one hand are four animals:
One „wie ein Löwe" / one "like a lion" / one «как лев» (verse 4),
one „gleich einem Bären" / one "like a bear" / one «похожий на медведя» (verse 5),
one „gleich einem Panther" / one "like a leopard" / one «как барс» (verse 6),
and „ein viertes Tier war furchtbar und schrecklich und sehr stark" / "a fourth beast, terrible and dreadful and exceedingly strong" / «зверь четвертый, страшный и ужасный и весьма сильный» (verse 7).

They all symbolize forms of government on earth without connections to God. They refer to all normal forms of human government.[66] May I remember a very important sentence by Winston Churchill. In the House of Commons in London he had said on November 11th 1947 that all political systems also have aspects of violence: "No one pretends that democracy is perfect or all-wise. Indeed, it has been said that democracy is the worst form of government except all those other forms that have been tried from time to time."[67]

On the other hand, the vision is speaking about a possibility of government against these earthly and human forms of government. It's expressed by a symbol: „einer wie eines Menschen Sohn" / "one like a son of man" / one «как бы Сын человеческий» (verse 13). And this symbol is realized and practiced by a new group of representatives on earth: „die Heiligen des Höchsten" / "the saints of the Most High" / the «святые Всевышнего» (verse 18). What group this might be? 28 years ago I had written: „Trotz aller Probleme bleibe ich dabei, dass hier keine Engelwesen gemeint sind, sondern auf eine von Gott akzeptierte irdische, menschliche Gruppe abgehoben wird: das erwählte Gottesvolk. Ich denke, dass auch die weitere Deutung dieses Begriffs in Dan 7 (vgl. die VV. 21.22.25.27) in diesem Horizont verbleibt, ja ihn noch klarer akzentuiert. Damit ist aber zugleich die Grundaussage des Textes als völlig unmessianisch verstanden. Diese Vision will keine kommende Rettergestalt ansagen, sondern sie symbolisiert den sich vollziehenden Wechsel der Herrschaftssysteme." An die Stelle des „eines wie eines Menschen Sohn" „treten die Mandatare der Herrschaft Gottes, nämlich die Personen Israels, die die wahrhaft menschliche Macht Gottes in seinem Auftrag gestalten werden." / "Besides of all problems I'm convinced that Daniel 7 does not speak about angels but about an earthly, human group, who is accepted by God: the Elected people of God. This means that the original message of our text was not messianic, was not speaking about a coming savior but wanted to symbolize a change of systems of power. Instead of the »one like a son of man« now a group of representatives of the government of God is envisioned, a group which will be the group of the persons of Israel: They will organize the really human power and government of God".[68]

---

[66] I refer to my book: Rainer Stahl: Von Weltengagement zu Weltüberwindung. Theologische Positionen im Danielbuch, Contributions to Biblical Exegesis and Theology 4, Kampen 1994, p. 53.
[67] Vgl.: https://de.wikiquote.org/wiki/Winston_Churchill (quoted on 11.1.2019).
[68] Cf.: Rainer Stahl, op. cit. (see note 65), p. 54 (the English translation I have given in a free formulation).

May I underline again what I have said: The animals are symbols of the present forms of governments of earth. And the „einer wie eines Menschen Sohn" / the "one like a son of man" / the one «как бы Сын человеческий» is originally a symbol of the expected fundamentally new form of government which only can come from heaven. This government then will be realized by persons from Israel, by Jews.

3.4.2. Presently we have many different manuscripts of the Greek translation of the Aramaic Book of Daniel. That's why different groups and generations have worked on the translation of this book. One detail is of special importance:

My German translation, the English translation, and your Russian translation say together that one „wie eines Menschen Sohn" / "one like a son of man" / one «как бы Сын человеческий» will come „mit den Wolken des Himmels" / "with the clouds of heaven" / «с облаками небесными» (verse 13a). But the original translation into the Greek language had written: „auf den Wolken des Himmels"[69] / "on the clouds of heaven" / «на облаках небесных». This very tiny change from "μετα" / „with" / «с» to "επι" / „on" / «на» shows that „επι" / „auf" / "on" / «на» identified the one „wie eines Menschen Sohn" / the one "like a son of man" / the one «как бы Сын человеческий» on the one hand and the „einer, der uralt war" / the "one that was ancient of days" / the «Ветхий днями» (verse 9) on the other hand! They both are described as experience of the <u>One God</u>!

And this new understanding we see in the New Testament in two sentences of the Gospel of Matthew:

| We will see „den Menschensohn kommen <u>auf</u> den Wolken des Himmels mit großer Kraft und Herrlichkeit" / | "the Son of man coming <u>on</u> the clouds of heaven with power and great glory" |

«и увидят Сына Человеческого,
грядущего <u>на</u> облаках небесных
с силою и славою великою»
(Matthäus / Matthew / Матфея 24:30b).

---

[69] Septuaginta Deutsch. Das griechische Alte Testament in deutscher Übersetzung, hg. Von Wolfgang Kraus und Martin Karrer, Stuttgart 2009, p. 1448.

And: „Von nun an werdet ihr sehen
den Menschensohn sitzend zur Rechten
der Kraft
und kommend <u>auf</u> den Wolken des Himmels"

"hereafter you will see
the Son of Man seated at the right hand
of Power,
and coming <u>on</u> the clouds of heaven"

«отныне у́зрите
Сына Человеческого, сидящего
одесную силы
и грядущего <u>на</u> облаках небесных»
(Matthäus / Matthew / Матфея 26,64a².b).

Again, we have seen that the messianic interpretation of this important text in Daniel 7 did happen in the time between the original Hebrew and Aramaic holy books and the theological foundation of the Christian church, from what the Gospel of Matthew is one important example.

4. Summary

4.1. We have to acknowledge that the messianic hopes in theology and devoutness in Judaism have been formulated in complicated processes – on the basis of the Hebrew and Aramaic holy texts mainly on the way of their translation into the Greek language.

4.2. Who sees in the hope of an "Anointed One", of a "Messiah", the revelation by God, he and she understands that the Spirit of God was working through the thinking and writing of Jewish and early Christian theologians.

4.3. A theology becomes a Christian one, when it interprets and understands Jesus of Nazareth as the "Anointed One", as the "Messiah", as the "Christ". When we want to remain as Christians then we have to keep this interpretation in mind. In all times, especially also today, we have to realize this interpretation in an exchange with the other religious hopes, especially with the hopes of the Jewish community.

In that connection I want to give a commentary: In Germany many interest groups organize metallic stones with the names of former Jewish neighbors, the "stumbling stones". They put these "stumbling stones" into the pavement of a single street in front of the door of the certain house, where these Jewish neighbors had lived, and from where they were deported and murdered in the Nazi time. When I see such a stone and read the name, then I always think: "How to pray?" I'm not a Jew; I'm a Christian. Because of that I think I can pray in the way what expresses the best hope from my side: "May the light of the almighty God shine upon you, and may you see God!" But I know that for a Jewish person all the dead are still waiting for the coming of the "Messiah", who had not yet come, that they still are waiting of this possibility to really seeing God!

4.4. Now we see that Jesus of Nazareth as "Christ" has fulfilled <u>and</u> altered many dimensions of the messianic hopes – for example by the way he was explained as a person who was able to fulfill miracles, who could heal sick persons, and finally he was explained as a person who is ready to go his way of suffering, to go to the cross. Therefore, a messianic theology which wants to be a Christian one will have its ground not simply in "old" texts but in the work of the Spirit of God in the time around the last years of BCE and the first years of CE. For the Christian messianic theology this period is <u>the</u> time of true revelation.

First Easter, then Christmas,
Text: Isaiah 9:1-7 / 8:23aβ – 9:6[70]

«Благодать Господа нашего Иисуса Христа, и любовь Бога Отца, и общение Святого Духа со свеми вами. Аминь.»	"The grace of our Lord Jesus Christ, the love of God and the fellowship of the Holy Spirit be with you all. Amen."

Дорогие Сёстры и Братья! Dear Sisters and Brothers!

Some time ago I have looked into old albums and have been reminded on things long time ago. 34 years they are ago: In those days I was working in the central office of the Lutheran World Federation (LWF) in the Ecumenical Centre in Geneva. In that summer I could serve the Seventh Assembly of the LWF in Budapest by taking minutes. Soon I should go back again into my home church. But this would not become an easy way back to Germany – as many may think now –, but a way back into my Thuringian home church, and this meant into the German Democratic Republic. In the beginning of February 1985, I arrived one evening in Jena: in front of the railway station darkness, coldness, many snow, no taxi near...

But from the end of November to the beginning of December 1984 I was delegated to a conference in Manila on the main island Luzon of the Philippines. During this trip I also had an interesting bus tour into the north of Luzon to Baguio, to visit there a church Centre. On my trip to Manila, I had visited Madras, today: Jennai, in southern India and Singapore, and on the way home even Japan. One thing was very surprising for me – especially in Japan: How intensively Christmas was celebrated in these non-Christian cultures. On the flight from Manila to Tokyo always Christmas hymns have been played – European Christmas songs! Why that? I really was surprised. In Tokyo in a shopping mall one huge Christmas tree! But what they do know there about the content of Christmas?

---

[70] This sermon I had sent as a gift to Christmas 2018. The German original was sent to the homepage of "Göttinger Predigten im Internet".

(In the shopping mall in Singapore. The photo was taken on November 30th, 1984.)

Especially impressive was this big window of a shopping mall in Singapore: No goods. But the background in blue with stares, one big star before it. Three tall figures of camels with riders in oriental cloths – walking westwards. And under the big star only five words: "Even wise men seek Jesus".

There has displayed a seller – maybe the owner of the shopping mall was a Christian – in the midst of the commercializing of Christmas the original message of this festivity! When and where we find such things today maybe in Germany?

Precisely this longing after the real content of the often emptied Christmas festivity is taken for this vesper, for this worship service on the eve before Christmas of tomorrow, is taken in the shape of a very old hope, which we find in the book of Isaiah:

«Народ, ходящий во тьме, увидит свет великий; на живущих в стране тени смертной – свет воссияет!» (Исаия / Isaiah 9:2).	"The people who walked in darkness have seen a great light; those who dwelt in a land of deep darkness, on them has light shined"

I said: A very old statement of hope. I have to add: An anonymous statement of hope, which might come from the state Israel and was brought by refugees after the destruction of Israel by the Assyrians in the 8th century before Christ into the state Judah, where it was incorporated into the traditional material of the Prophet of Judah and Jerusalem, Isaiah. This means: Already the word itself and its oldest history explain that injustice is on work. This word, what describes geographically the state of Israel (not the state of Judah) in a precise and short form, is protesting against this injustice. It is therefore a prophetical protest <u>and</u> a prophetical statement of hope in one:

«Прежнее время умалило землю Завулонову и землю Неффалимову; но последующее возвеличит приморский путь, за-Иорданскую страну, Галилею языческую» (Исаия / Isaiah 9:1).	"In the former time he brought into contempt the land of Zebulun and the land of Naphtali, but in the latter time he will make glorious the way of the sea, the land beyond the Jordan, Galilee of the nations"

Now I would like to document an interesting insight. For some it would not belong to a sermon, but it demonstrates that the biblical words "are not only words to read, as many think, but real words to live" – like Martin Luther had explained in his letter from July 1st, 1530, in which he had sent his interpretation of Psalm 118 to Friedrich Pistorius in Nuremberg. Because the bible was not transferred in a stupid way but always actively transmitted – like we are now searching for the Christmas message in our year 2018: As the Egyptian Jews in the 2nd century before Christ translated the book of Isaiah into Greek, produced the Septuagint, they kept the sequence from the eighth to the ninth chapter. This shows my edition of the Septuagint by Alfred Rahlfs.[71] But the translators of this Bible into German in our 21st century after Christ have ordered these verses in a new way: The last part of Isaiah 8:23 stands now already under Isaiah 9:1.[72] But there these translators only have shown what already the "Revised Standard Version" of the English Bible from 1611 and the Russian Bible («Синодальная Библия») from 1873 have done! When I translated this sermon into English and incorporated the Bible quotes in Russian language then I realized one very important fact: In the English Bible ("Revised Standard Version") and also in the Russian Bible chapter 8 only has 22 verses, and the just quoted text is the first verse of chapter 9!

---

[71] See: Alfred Rahlfs (Ed.); Septuaginta II, 2. Auflage, 1935, Stuttgart 1965, p. 577.
[72] See: Wolfgang Kraus and Martin Karrer: Septuaginta Deutsch, Stuttgart 2009, p. 1238.

Now we stop: The advertisement in Singapore has taken the large hope of "light" – and interpreted it into direction of the Centre of the Christian faith, of Jesus. It forces us to recognize Jesus in one of this old prophetical word:

«Ибо младенец родился нам;	"For to us a child is born,
Сын дан нам;	to us a son is given;
владычество на раменах Его;	and the government will be upon his shoulder,
и нарекут имя Ему:	and his name will be called
Чудный, Советник, Бог крепкий,	»Wonderful Counsellor, Mighty God,
Отец вечностей, Князь мира»	Everlasting Father, Prince of Peace«"
(Исаия / Isaiah 9:6).	

Now the Jewish translators from the 2nd century before Christ have really changed our biblical word: "and his name is called «messanger of great decisions«; because I will bring peace over the rulers, peace and health for him".[73] This exciting form are not kept and given whether in the Russian Bible – what could be expected – nor in the English Bible. Why? One reason could be the fact that in our New Testament this old prophetical word is taken twice: In the letter to the Ephesians 2:14: «Ибо Он есть мир наш» / "For he is our peace", and by the Evangelist Luke in the hymn of the angels in the Christmas story, Luke 2:14: «и на земле мир, в человеках благоволение» / "and on earth peace among men with whom he is pleased"!

Our text for the sermon of this Christmas Eve binds this big hope of peace back to a fundamental longing, to difficult and exciting words! These we have to realize first – without immediate identification of the announced person with Jesus. We have first to understand this announced person from the content of the old prophetical word, from the exciting diagnosis of fundamental changes in society and politics, from changes, with what the newly born originally is not engaged, which occur before his birth or parallel to his birth – and I only take some central terms:

«Он будет веселиться пред Тобою,	"They rejoice before thee
как веселятся во время жатвы,	as with joy at the harvest,
как радуются при разделе добычи.	as men rejoice when they divide the spoil.
Ибо ярмо, тяготившее его, […]	For the yoke of his burden, […]
сокрушишь как в день Мадиама.»	thou hast broken as on the day of Midian"
(Исаия / Isaiah 9:3b-4).	

---

[73] See: Alfred Rahlfs, op. cit. (see note 71), p. 578, and: Wolfgang Kraus and Martin Karrer, op. cit. (see note 72), p.1239.

Now big hopes are proclaimed as reality for the «приморский путь» / "the way of the sea", for the «за-Иорданская страна» / "the land beyond the Jordan", for the «Галилея языческая» / "Galilee of the nations", for the «народ, ходящий во тьме» / "The people who walked in darkness", for the «живущие в стране тени смертной» / "those who dwelt in a land of deep darkness": Its suffering under war and crime will be brought to an end! We will think of the innocent people in Syria and in the Ukraine!

There we realize, what for a new time our prophetical word is describing, is proclaiming. Therefore, there is only one solution to identify the person who will bring all these changes –

«Он возвеличит приморский путь.	"He will make glorious the way of the sea.
Ибо ярмо, тяготившее его,	For the yoke of his burden,
[...] сокрушишь [...]	[...] thou hast broken [...]
Ибо [...] одежда обагренная кровию,	For [...] every garmet rolled in blood
будут отданы на сожжение,	will be burned as fuel
в пищу огню» –:	for the fire" –:

God himself will do all of this! God will bring the liberation to all of his people in need, the liberation to all in need!

And now – дорогие Сёстры и Братья, dear Sisters and Brothers – we have realized the challenge when we relate this prophetical word to Christmas, this means: to Jesus of Nazareth – like our Christian tradition is doing this:

Before and during the birth of Jesus all these changes have not occurred. Even in the shape of the tradition that Herod should have ordered a liquidation of small boys in the area of Bethlehem (only given in Matthew 2:16-18) a new victory of the «одежда обагренная кровию» / "every garmet rolled in blood" is shown. Even, in the shape of the report about the process against Jesus and about his killing (see only Matthew 26,47 – 27,61) the terrible message is given, that this «Чудный, Советник» / "Wonderful Counsellor", that this «Бог крепкий» / "Mighty God", that this «Отец вечностий» / "Everlasting Father", that this «Князь мира» / "Prince of Peace" seemed not to be successful!

How we can find a Christmas message? From our old prophetical word a Christmas message? There is only one way: To relate to a huge challenge. But from this all is dependent. Only all who realize this huge challenge, and agree with it, understand it within the depth of their existence as true – traditionally we say:

"believe it" –, only all these people are able to "understand" the importance of Christmas, are able to say together with the seller in Singapore: „Even wise men seek Jesus." These are all persons who believe the crucified as the resurrected one:

«Не бойтесь, ибо знаю,	"Do not be afraid; for I know
что вы ищете Иисуса распятого;	that you seek Jesus who was crucified.
Его нет здесь:	He is not here;
Он воскрес, как сказал!»	for he has risen, as he said"
(Матфея / Matthew 28:5b-6).	

Beginning with Easter it can become Christmas for us! Keep on this faith even in 2018 and in 2019! It helps us to manage our life. From Easter we can express our trust in faith – as I want to express it now with words of a hymn in the hymn book of the community of Herrnhut:

„ Peace what no storm may destroy,	„Friede, den kein Sturm zerstört,
Word what is listening to our words,	Wort, das unsre Worte hört,
Truth what is thinking of the blind,	Wahrheit, die an Blinde denkt,
Love that offers itself,	Liebe, die sich selbst verschenkt,
Heaven that loves the earth [...].	Himmel, der die Erde liebt [...].
Praise the power that bows down.	Lobt die Macht, die sich verneigt.
Praise the heaven that is not silent.	Lobt den Himmel, der nicht schweigt.
Praise the light that is lightened within us.	Lobt das Licht, in uns entfacht.
Light from light within our night"	Licht aus Licht in unsrer Nacht"
	(Georg Schmid).

Amen.

«И мир Божий,	"And the peace of God
который превыше всякого ума,	which passes all understanding,
соблюдёт сердца ваши	will keep your hearts
и помышления ваши	and your minds
во Христе Иисусе!»	in Christ Jesus."

"I will make a covenant of peace with them", Bodelschwingh-House, Erlangen[74]

"The grace of our Lord Jesus Christ, and the love of God and the fellowship of the Holy Spirit be with you all." Amen.

«Благодать Господа нашего Иисуса Христа, и любовь Бога Отца, и общение Святого Духа со всеми вами». Аминь.

Dear Sisters and Brothers! Дорогие Сёстры и Братья!

First, we have been listening to the old known and the beloved and the expected story of Christmas from the Gospel of Luke: That night of the birth of Jesus Christ we do remember over all our old world. On that way we remember something totally new – a gospel which is coming from the heavenly world into our earthly world:

"For to you is born this day in the city of David a Saviour, who is Christ the Lord […] »Glory to God in the highest and on earth peace among men with whom he is pleased«" / «Ибо ныне родился вам в городе Давидовом Спасиель, Который есть Христос Господь […] „Слава в вышних Богу, и на земле мир, в человеках баговоление"» (Luke / Лук 2:11.14).

Additionally, I quote a hope from the Book of Ezekiel (which is the Bible text for the sermon for the holy night this year) which you may never have read or heard until now – a fundamental hope for the Holy Land:

"My servant David shall be king over them; and they shall all have one shepherd. They shall follow my ordinances and be careful to observe my statutes. They shall dwell in the land […] that I gave to my servant Jacob […]; and David my servant shall be their prince for ever. I will make a covenant of peace with them" / «А раб Мой Давид будет Царем над ними и Пастырем всех их, и они будут ходить в заповедях Моих и уставы Мои будут соблюдать и выполнять их. И будут жить на земле, которую Я дал рабу Моему Иакобу […] и раб Мой Давид будет князем у них вечно. И заключу с ними завет мира» (Ezekiel / Иезекииль 37:24.25a.d.26a).

---

[74] This meditation was given in the house for elderly people in Erlangen, in the Bodelschwingh-House, in the morning of December 24th, 2019, and it was also written to friends in Russia.

This text produces a surprising idea about this area in the Near East, about this area of the present states of Israel, Palestine, Jordan, Syria and Lebanon: That a new responsible person, a successor of David, will realize justice and compassion for the society, because he will bring up new economic and ecological situations!

And the fulfilling of all of these hopes is expressed in the Gospel of Luke because of the birth of Jesus Christ. But not simply within the daily life and not simply for everyone – but as fulfilling of a truth, which is coming from the heavenly world: "Glory to God in the highest and on earth peace among men with whom he is pleased." / «Слава в вышних Богу, и на земле мир, в человеках баговоление»!

As Christians we underline these great and fascinating hopes as truth within our worship services, within our nativity plays, also within our festivity here in the Bodelschwingh-House, and additionally within our families between parents and children, between our families and friends and guests. Like I have a very important remembrance from my childhood: Often to Holy Eve in our apartment also an old lady, a friend of my grandmother was our guest – Charlotte Coudray, with a prename we know from the time of Goethe! Her visit always was for me a realistic experience of this big word over the Holy Night: "Glory to God in the highest and on earth peace among men with whom he is pleased." / «Слава в вышних Богу, и на земле мир, в человеках баговоление»! And now I have to add from the Book of Ezekiel: "I will make a covenant of peace with them" / «И заключу с ними завет мира»!

Even in times of war soldiers have tried to build signs of this truth of the Holy Night – for example precisely 105 years ago, on December 24th and 25th 1914 at the western frontline between German and British soldiers within the First World War. Even officers had organized these signs of friendship between the soldiers across the frontline!

For me these signs of friendship are wonderful signs of the Christmas hope of a better world. But additionally, I know that these signs of a better world are shaped within the normal world, even within a terrible reality of a war in those days! Our world, our society is until now marked by suffering, by injustice, by inequality. Those experiences oppose all of our Christmas festivities! Even now our worship service here in the Bodelschwingh-House is opposing those daily suffering, daily fear within our lives – even within our house!

But those signs are very important for us – and we remain realistic with such signs. What we have heard from the old text of the Book of Ezekiel for the Judean society never would fulfilled, even so some positive results within the society of the state of Israel could have been managed: For all Judean and Jewish societies these hopes refer to the future! The same is the fact for our Christian communities – especially during all our Christmas festivities: This hope means a reality in a wonderful future: "My servant David shall be king over them; and they shall all have one shepherd. They shall follow my ordinances and be careful to observe my statutes" / «А раб Мой Давид будет Царем над ними и Пастырем всех их, и они будут ходить в заповедях Моих и уставы Мои будут соблюдать и выполнять их»!

Today we're thinking about and we're celebrating the birth of Jesus Christ. Today we're thanking for this birth. With all of it we know: This wonderful beginning of "Glory" / «Слава» and "Peace" / «Мир» we're connected with Jesus, we're expecting finally only from him, from Jesus. Additionally, we're ready bearing this wonderful hope into our society, into our world. And this will only be real within very small beginnings! – Today, on this day of the holy night very openly, but in other days only in a hidden way!

Jochen Klepper, a poet from the 30th years of the former century, has described this tension in his "Christmas song in the war" in a wonderful way. I'm not clear whether I can really translate this song; but I will try it:

„Nun ruht doch alle Welt.	"All world is now resting.
O Herz, wie willst du's fassen?	O heart, can you understand?
Die Erde liegt im Streit,	The Earth is in conflict,
von allem Heil verlassen,	departed from all salvation,
ist friedlos weit und breit	near and far without peace
und wider dich gestellt.	and in opposition against you.
Doch der die Erde schuf,	Even, who created the world
hat deine Angst gesehen	has recognized your fear
und hat sich aufgemacht,	and has started to come,
will dir zur Seite stehen,	wants to stay besides you
ein Helfer voller Macht.	as a helper full power.
Hell klingt sein Friedensruf.	Clear is his call for peace.

[...]

Die Tannen freuen sich.	The firs are happy.
Die Hürden auf dem Felde	The hurdles on the fields
erhellt ein klarer Schein.	enlightened by a clear glow.
Komm, Engel, komm und melde:	Come, angle, come and report:
Was bricht zur Nacht herein?	What is beginning in that night?
Kommst du und meinst auch mich?	Are you coming and also thinking of me?
Gott Lob! In deinem Licht	God praise! Within your Light
darf ich das Licht erschauen,	I'm allowed to recognize the Light,
das Kind, den Herrn der Welt!	the child, the Lord of the world!
Ihm will ich mich vertrauen,	Him I want to trust,
Er ist es, der mich hält	He is that one, who is keeping me
und rettet im Gericht."	and is saving within the court."[75]

This Christmas Message – "Glory to God in the highest and on earth peace among men with whom he is pleased." / «Слава в вышних Богу, и на земле мир, в человеках баговоление» and additionally "I will make a covenant of peace with them" / «И заключу с ними завет мира» –, this Christmas Message is called above and remembered even against our sorrows, our fears, our sicknesses, our pains, our brokenness and our suffering. Also today, also on the Christmas Eve of the year 2019 here in the Bodelschwingh-House! Again, with the words by Jochen Klepper:

> "Even, who created the world
> has recognized your fear
> and has started to come,
> wants to stay besides you
> as a helper full power.
> Clear is his call for peace."

Amen.

"And the peace of God,	«И мир Божий,
which passes all our understanding,	который превыше всякого ума,
may keep your hearts and minds	соблюдёт сердца ваши
in Christ Jesus, our Lord!" Amen.	во Христе Иисусе». Аминь.

---

[75] Jochen Klepper: Kyrie. Geistliche Lieder, [15]1968, p. 36.38.

Jesus Christ is the true Sun,
Text: Luke 2:1-17[76]

Dear Sisters and Brothers!

About Christmas we all have been reflecting often: Christmas is one of the most known festivals for us. During this festival we really feel at home. I'm sure that we all remember Christmas festivals in our home – as we have been children. For me one remembrance is of special importance: My parents liked to introduce an old lady – the friend of my grandmother. We called her: "Aunt Lotte". I still see how she was ironing the fine gift ribbons from the gift packages at the warm tiled stove – from the gift packages, what my grandma had sent us from West Germany. That we could use them again next year for the coming Christmas…

Therefore, I want to start today a little bit unfamiliar:

A scholar – Dionysius Exiguus – had developed time tables approximately in the year 525 after Christ. There he identified as the birthday of Jesus December 25th of 753 "ab urbe condita" / "after the founding of the town Rome".[77]

753 before Christ is the traditional founding year of Rome, the capital of the Roman Empire. This means that Jesus was born after these 753 years – in the year 1 after Christ, the year 0 does not exist in our time calculation.

I've understood: All writers of the antiquity who mentioned Jesus in their works never have reflected about his birth. The only source we have are the different statements in our New Testament. What we get when we connect these statements with this calculation?

The first and very serious statement we find in the Gospel of Luke, chapter 3: "In the fifteenth year of the reign of Tiberius Caesar, Pontius Pilate being governor of Judea, and Herod being tetrarch of Galilee, and his brother Philipp tetrarch of the region of Ituraea and Trachonitis […], the Word of God came to John the son of Zechariah in the wilderness" (verses 1-2).

---

[76] This sermon was given in the Bodelschwingh-House in Erlangen on December 24th, 2021. The English version was sent to friends in Russia.
[77] See: Alden A. Mosshammer: Art: "Chronologie IV: Christliche Zeitrechnung", RGG⁴, Volume 2, Tübingen 1999, Col. 356-360, here: Col. 359.

There the baptism of Jesus as approximately 30 years old man by John the Baptist is ordered into the 15th governmental year of Emperor Tiberius. According to our time calculation we come into the year 28 / 29 after Christ.[78] This statement means that Jesus was born between the years 2 before Christ and 1 after Christ.[79] We can also say: 2021 years ahead of us!

The second statement we find in the Gospel of Matthew, chapter 2:
"Now when Jesus was born in Bethlehem of Judea in the days of Herod the king, behold, wise men from the East came to Jerusalem, saying, «Where is he who has been born king of the Jews? For we have seen his star in the East, and have come to worship him»" (verses 1-2).

What is told? Men who are scientists about the sky and the stars have come from Babylon to Jerusalem and are asking the King Herod after a new born king. This King Herod is normally identified with King Herod the Great.[80] But he died according to our time calculation in the year 4 before Christ. Because of that I learned already during my study time: We do not know precisely in what year Jesus was born. We only can say: In the last governmental years of this King Herod – may be in the year 6 before Christ.[81] We can also say: 2027 years ahead of us!

And the third statement we had heard as I had read the Gospel of today – the statement in the Gospel of Luke, chapter 2:
"In those days a decree went out from Caesar Augustus that all the world should be enrolled. This was the first enrolment, when Quirinius was governor of Syria" (verses 1-2).

---

[78] See: Friedrich Wilhelm Horn: Art. Tiberius, RGG⁴, Volume 8, Tübingen 2005, Col. 395.
[79] See: Uwe Jochum: In der Mitte der Zeit. Die neue Chronologie des Lebens Jesu [In the centre of the time. The new chronology of the life of Jesus], Hildesheim, Zürich, New York 2021, p. 12-15. Uwe Jochum understands the statement in Luke 3 as the most credible one: „Der von Lukas gebotene Synchronismus ist historisch korrekt und markiert den lokalen zeitgeschichtlichen Hintergrund für den öffentlichen Auftritt von Johannes dem Täufer im 15. Regierungsjahr des Kaisers Tiberius" / "The synchronism given by Luke is historic correct and shows the local background of the time for the open work of John the Baptist in the 15th governmental year of Emperor Tiberius" (p. 14).
[80] Uwe Jochum, op. cit. (see note 79), p. 61-63, discusses who are the King Herod might be, who are mentioned in the Gospel of Mathew. His result: Not King Herod the Great, but his son Herod Archelaos: „Zur Zeit von Herodes Archelaos, dem »König« von Judäa, wurde Johannes gezeugt und geboren; Jesus hingegen, der noch während der Regierungszeit des Archelaos gezeugt worden war, wurde erst während des Steuerzensus des Quirinius geboren" / "In the time of Herod Archelaos, the »King« of Judea, John was conceived and born, but Jesus who was conceived in the governmental time of Archelaos was born during the tax census of Quirinius". (p. 63).
[81] See again: Uwe Jochum, op. cit. (see note 79), p. 11.

About both persons we know very well, when they were working: Emperor Augustus was governing from 44 before Christ until the year 14 after Christ, and he died in this year.[82] And Quirinius was in the year 6 / 7 after Christ the imperial Legate / Governor in Syria.

But one information, which Luke is giving to us, we have to correct: The enrolment was not for the whole Roman Empire but one for the until now independent Judea and Samaria. After the deposition of the duke there – of Archelaos, one son of King Herod the Great – these provinces belonged then to the province of Syria. And because of that an enrolment in this new territory was necessary.

Luke suggests that Jesus was born in the period from the year 6 to the year 7 after Christ. We can also say: 2015 years ahead of us![83]

I'm convinced that Jesus really was alive – because we have within the New Testament different dates for his birth. Against the thesis of atheists that Jesus never has existed,[84] I'm forced to say: Jesus has really existed. We do not know his precise birthday, but we are able to remember his birth today – at the Christmas festival!

As the scholar, may be in 525 after Christ, identified December 25th as the birthday of Jesus many other influences were important – not only the statements in Luke 2 and 3. Very important was that in the Roman culture December 25th was the festival of the victorious sun.

A Christian theologian of that time had written: "The pagans were used to celebrate at December 25th the festival of the birthday of the sun and inflamed fires in honor of this festival. [...] Because the teachers of the church saw that the

---

[82] See: Gerhard Binder: Art. "Augustus", RGG⁴, Volume 1, Tübingen 1998, Col. 973-974.
[83] See: Daniel R. Schwarz: Art. "Herodes/Herodeshaus", RGG⁴, Band 3, Tübingen 2000, Col. 1675-1677, and: Jürgen Schefzyk / Wolfgang Zwickel (ed.): Judäa und Jerusalem – Leben in römischer Zeit, Katholisches Bibelwerk, Stuttgart 2010, p. 57-58.
Uwe Jochum, op. cit. (see note 79), p. 53-61, discussed Luke 2 in the following way: He identifies the birth day of Jesus at the end of the year 6 or in the beginning of the year 7 after Christ. The enrolment for Judea and Samara was for him in the year from September 6 to September 7.
[84] See: „Neue Zweifel an der historischen Existenz Jesu" / "New doubts at the historical existence of Jesus" on the Homepage of the „humanistischen Pressedienstes" (vom 30.9.2011):
https://hpd.de/node/12044 (seen at November 25th, 2021) and the information to „Neuen Atheismus" / "New Atheism" in the paper on the „Jesus-Mythos": https://de.wikipedia.org/wiki/Jesus-Mythos (seen at November 25th, 2021).

Christians were interested in this festival, they ordered that at this day should be celebrated the festival of the true birth."[85]

As we Christians have adapted this festival of the sun and identified it with the birthday of Jesus, we have expressed our deep believe that Jesus Christ is the true sun which is giving us life. He is the true light which is shining us in deep night.

Because of that the shepherds had realized the "an angel of the Lord appeard to them, and the glory of the Lord shone around them" (Luke 2:9).
Because of that the wise men have seen the star and have gone to his birthplace: "For we have seen his star in the East" (Matthew 2:2).
We are happy about burning candles and understand them as a sign of the light which has come into the world through Christ.

As I was pastor in Altenburg one time I have visited a member of my congregation in the intensive care unit in the hospital – may be in the year 1987 – and I had celebrated communion together with this lady. I had not asked but only put the cross and two candles on her bed cabinet and I had lighted the candles. Without I knew whether this would be good for her or not. But the nurse told to me after it: "It was like Christmas!"

There a light is shining in the darkness. What I say: one light? Many candles – lighted as symbols of the light Jesus Christ!

May also we may become able to light for others! This wants to be the Christmas message for us this year: We may understand us as a kind of "Moon". Each one of us as a small "Moon": We let us lighted by the sun Jesus Christ. And then we are lighting in a new way. All the shadows of our fear and suffering, of our pain and our loneliness are outshined by the light with which Christ lights us!

Christmas in this year 2021 means: We open us for this light. We become thankful for this light.
And then Christmas means in this year 2021: We light now for others with this light, what we have received.

---

[85] I refer to a book from GDR-times which I still like to use: Georg von Gynz-Rekowski: Der Festkreis des Jahres, Berlin ²1985, p. 33. But the author does not inform what Syriac theologian had made this statement.

A first step might be: To say "Thank you". Better a little bit to much instead of to less.

A second step might be: Instead of difficulties to show happiness. To give smiling.

May be this Christmas festival of the year 2021 become without parallel for us on this way – and for the people around us.
Amen

"You are right, Teacher", Чебоксары / Tscheboksary, Mark 12:28-34[86]

Дорогие Сёстры и Братья! Dear Sisters and Brothers!

В нашей церкви в Германии сегодня это «Израиль Воскресенье». Это очень важно подумать о соответствии между Еврейство и Христианство, между Синагога и Церковь! / In our churches in Germany we are celebrating today the "Israel Sunday". It is very important to reflect about the relations between Jews and Christians, between the Synagogue and the Church!

You may imagine why this is important for us as Germans, for us as Christians within Germany! But even for other peoples is this very important – that they become aware of the dangers in this connection: Some time ago I have read in a newspaper that still today in the far east of Poland there would exist the tradition to blame the Jewish neighbors as even today responsible for the crucifixion of Jesus. That's terrible nonsense. May I tell you that there exists a very interesting and wonderful poem by Martin Luther with which he had reinterpreted an old poem from the Middle Age. And this revised poem was published in the year 1544. May I try to translate it into the English language, but I also read the German original:

"Our great sin and heavy misery
has beaten Jesus, the true son of God,
at the cross.
Therefore, we should not accuse you
as enemies
you, the poor Judas,
and the Jewish community.
The guilt is ours already!
Kyrie – be gracious to us!"

„Unsere große Sünde und schwere Missetat
Jesus, den wahren Gottessohn,
ans Kreuz geschlagen hat.
Dazu wir dich armer Judas,
dazu der Juden Schar
nicht feindlich dürfen schelten.

Die Schuld ist unser gar.
Kyrie eleison."

Against this background we hear today our biblical text from the Gospel of Mark for the sermon! This is a wonderful statement in favor of the deep continuity between us, the Christians, to our Jewish ancestors and also neighbors. Two sentences at the end of our biblical word are important. The Jewish theologian says

---

[86] This sermon was given in the Lutheran congregation of Tscheboksary in Russia on August 25th, 2019.

to Jesus: «Хорошо, Учитель! Истину сказал Ты» / "You are right, Teacher; you have truly said [...]" (Verse 32). And the Jew Jesus says to the theologian: «Недалеко Ты от Царствия Божия» / "You are not far from the kingdom of God" (Verse 34).

These sentences are very important. Because Jesus has given this evaluation not only for this theologian in the first century but also for us in the 21st century – in Germany and also for you in Russia and here in Tscheboksary. It is important to listen to the Jewish heritage, to the Old Testament – even, what is additionally important, to the first part of the Hebrew Bible, to the Torah. Jesus has given us two quotes – one from the book of Второзаконие / Deuteronomy and the other from the book of Левит / Leviticus.

I'm doing my preparation for a sermon always in the following way: I'm writing by hand the most important sentences of the biblical text for the sermon on a paper – but in the original language – Greek or Hebrew. And then I reflect about the meaning for me, the meaning for us, the meaning for you. And soon I can start to make first notes. Mostly the pencil – I'm always working at first hand with a pencil –, mostly the pencil is marching quickly above the paper.

But in our case in my first step – copying important sentences – I have not only written the most important quotes of Mark 12 in Greek language. I added immediately the Hebrew original. For the first answer by Jesus even without looking into the Hebrew Bible, because this sentence is such famous: «שמע ישראל יהוה אלהינו יהוה אחד!» / «Слушай Израиль: Господь, Бог наш, Господь един есть.» / "Hear, O Israel: The Lord our God is one Lord." (Второзаконие / Deuteronomy 6:4). And now I have to change your Russian Bible and also the English Bible, because the original wording means two sentences: «Господь есть Бог наш!» / "The Lord is our God!" and: «Господь единый есть!» / "The Lord is unique!" (cf. verse 29 in Mark 12).

But for the second sentence of Jesus I had to look into the book of Левит, into the book Levitikus 19:18: «וְאָהַבְתָּ לְרֵעֲךָ כָּמוֹךָ!» / «Возлюби ближнего твоего как самого себя!» / "you shall love your neighbour as yourself!" (cf. verse 31 in Mark 12).

In the beginning I had made the statement that you may imagine why this Sunday is important for us as Germans. I only want to give one example, but an important one: SS-men, who have done service in Auschwitz, have witnessed that many Jews have died by proclaiming this very statement from the book of

Второзаконие / Deuteronomy. And I think that this witness is really valid, because they did not understand and therefore only could express in a very vague form what they had heard: »שמע ישראל יהוה אלהינו יהוה אחד!« – «Слушай Израиль! Господь есть Бог наш! Господь единый есть!» / "Hear, O Israel: The Lord is our God! The Lord is unique!" What they – these SS-men – would have done if they would have been true and convinced Christians? First, they could not have become SS-men. That's clear. But reflect on this question!

That's very important. Because this statement of the Bible also is our confession: We believe in one God. God is only and one. We Christians experience this one and only God on three ways – as Father, as Son and as Holy Spirit. But all of these ways, all of these personalities lead us to the only and one God. He is – what we as Christians from Germany and you from Russia and from the people of Ingria are able to say –, he is our God, who is the only and one God!

Please go together with me one step back: Who receives qualities like a God today? I think of the modern culture of communication and influence in "Facebook" and in "Instagram" and so on: to become an "influencer" and to find many "followers". I do not participate in that culture. But what I see sometimes in TV or in newspapers show me that for many "followers" the "influencer" becomes a little bit like a deity. There we have to be careful. We may take ideas from others. But we never should acknowledge these others like deities. The best help would be to believe in the true and only God. This liberates us from being bound to humans or to things.

And: All who join this belief – also you here in Tscheboksary – establish a relation of love, of deep responsibility and obedience to this God and to their neighbors! That you are here in our worship service shows that you try love God. And then reflect about your neighbor here in the congregation and also in your street and in your house and say to yourself: What responsibility I could take for whom of them?

That we try to love our neighbor is also a way to becoming free, to becoming liberated. Now we are liberated from ourselves; now I'm liberated from myself. Normally for each of us the own situation is in the Centre. This changes when we have a child, when we have become mother or father. Then this girl, this boy occupies the first rank in our life. And this becomes also possible in direction to my neighbor. Who is this «רֵעָה», who is this «ближний», who is the »neighbour«? First this is the «друг мой» / »my friend«, the «товарищ мой» / »my comrade«, it is the person who lives next to me, with whom I'm working, who I meet in my daily life.

Here one story becomes important which Jesus has told in connection with our scene. But not in the gospel of Mark, but in the gospel of Luke. There our story is told with another color than in the gospel of Mark. In the gospel of Luke the theologian is asking Jesus: «А кто мой ближний?» / "And who is my neighbor?" (Luke 10:29). And there Jesus is telling the famous story of the Samaritan who has gone far beyond all borders and helped the injured Jewish man. This horizon is also very important.

Therefore, I send you with the following question into the new week: For whom I could take responsibility? Or: What responsibility I could take for whom of my neighbors?
Amen.

The sixth supplication of the Lord's Prayer: God, the Father, does for us the good.[87]

Until Advent 1st, 2018, there was a discussion in the Roman-Catholic Church about the understanding of the sixth supplication of the Lord's Prayer: What God is doing with us? In the French and in the Italian language they have changed the formulation away from God as tempting us to God as testing, as proving us. Even the French speaking Lutheran congregation in Moscow did follow this decision. Therefore, this paper goes the following way: We have to understand the difficult dimensions seeing God as Father and Mother (Pope John Paul I.). This was done for a long time, what the personal names in the Bible show. One important story of the New Testament is that one of the "lost Son" and his relation to his father (Luke 15). Against this background we have to question the formulation that God "does not lead us into temptation". First we have to understand that God does not tempt us – see: James 1. And important is here the statement of the Apostle Paul in 1. Corinthians 10: "God is faithful"! We as Lutherans have a very clear insight by Martin Luther in his Small Catechism: "God does not tempt anyone – but we're asking in that prayer that God may save us from all bad powers […], that we may win and get the victory." Therefore I'm still praying the Lord's Prayer with the traditional formulation. But I understand it in the reflected way: Within our lifetime God does not tempt but does prove us!

Keywords: Lord's Prayer, God as Father and mother, sixth supplication, temptation, testing, proving, Pope Francis, Martin Luther, Small Catechism

1. A language picture for God: "Father" / Изображение языка для Бога: «Отец»

1.1. I think we may suppose that most Christians are praying the Lord's Prayer every day. Are they still surprised that they are addressing God as "father"?

---

[87] This paper first was given on March 20th, 2019, in Kerkhofen, pastorat Sulzbürg near Neumarkt (Oberpfalz), in a broader form. In a shorter version it was given in June 2019 to persons who prepare themselves to service in the congregation in Braşov / Kronstadt and to a group of Hungarian Pastors in Tarlungeni / Tatrang (both in Romania), and finally to congregational groups on August 20th in Moscow, on August 22nd in Saransk, on August 24th in Tscheboksary and on August 27th in Birsk (in Russia). And it was published in the Almanach "Religion. Church. Society, Research and Publications in the Field of Theology and Religious Studies, Volume IX, Saint Petersburg 2020, p. 86-98.

1.1.1. This way to address God leads the praying person into the Centre of the relation to the parents and also to the children: Does someone remembers the parents together with conflicts or in a peaceful way? Do the children remember their parents together with conflicts or in a peaceful way? Have they become self-reliant? Or are they still in the feeling of being guided by their parents? Have the parents set their children free or do they still bind them to themselves and try to govern them in all questions? By reflecting about all of this we realize that the way to address God as "father" also may create problems.

1.1.2. I give two modern quotes by Popes – one positive, one explaining problems: On September 10th, 1978, Pope John Paul I. said: „E' papa; più ancora è madre" – "God is father and even more he is mother."[88] And in our days Pope Francis had said: "Today we have reached a point where our society has to be called as 'a society without fathers'. In our western culture the figure of the father is more or less absent. [...] This creates wounds in the life of our children and youngsters. Their problems are also related to this missing [...] of nearness and good examples."[89]

But, when I had given this lecture before, people also have criticized the evaluation by Pope Francis and said: Many fathers take their responsibility in a new and good way. This is also part of our time.

1.2. To address God as a "father" is not just an idea of us. Instead: In the history of religions the addressing of God as a "father" is nearly universal![90] One example for this common practice we see in personal names in the Bible:

1.2.1. Now we have to realize that all biblical names are sentences. They show what the parents wanted to say about their children or what the parents are ordered how to give the child a name. I remind one important example: «и наречешь Ему имя: Иисус; ибо Он спасет людей Своих от грехов их» / "and you shall call his name Jesus, for he will save his people from their sins" (Матфея / Matthew 1:21). Why this could be said? What the name «Иисус» has to do with the possibility of saving the people? We only understand this when we know what «Иисус» means in Hebrew: יֵשׁוּעַ – Jeschuʿah, in a long form: יְהוֹשֻׁעָה – Jᵉhoschuʿah.

---

[88] https://de.wikipedia.org/Johannes_Paul_I. (again read on June 13th, 2020).
[89] Papst Franziskus: Vaterunser. Das Gebet Jesu neu gelesen, München 2018, p. 18s.20 (The translation into English was made by myself).
[90] See: Rainer Neu: „Vatername Gottes, I. Religionsgeschichtlich", RGG⁴, Vol. 8, 2005, Cl. 889.

This term means: "Jahwe / God is the savior!" Therefore, the quoted sentence could have been written in the Gospel according to Matthew.

1.2.2. And two names are of special interest: אֲבִיָּה and אֲבִיָּהוּ – 'Abijjah and 'Abijjahu – the first means: "My father is Jah", the second means: "My father is Jahu" ("Jah" and "Jahu" are short forms of the name of God: "Jahwe"). I refer to the king Abija of Judah, who governed during the end of the 10th century, maybe until 908 before Christ (cf. 3. Царств / 1. Kings 15). This name shows: There was already in very old times the possibility to call the God of Israel and of Judah as father of a man – may be especially by a name of a king. But generally we could say: There we have the belief that this God might be the "father" of us humankind. See also the two prophetical words in the book of Isaiah:

«Только Ты – Отец наш [...]; Ты, Господи – Отец наш, от века имя Твоё: 'Искупитель наш'» / "For thou art our Father [...]; thou, O Lord, art our Father, our Redeemer from of old is thy name" (Исаия / Isaiah 63:16).
«Но ныне, Господи, Ты – Отец наш; мы [...] дело руки Твоей» / "Yet, O Lord, thou art our Father; [...] we are all the work of thy hand" (Исаия / Isaiah 64:8).
The authors of these words in the Book of Isaiah speak of God as their "father" and express the insight that they are his work, express the faith that he has created them.

1.3.1. This conviction has become fundamental and really basic in the Christian relation to God. The reason was the relation to God which Jesus has had, which he has expressed, which he has proclaimed in his deeds and in his preaching. There I remember only the story of the "lost Son" in the Gospel of Luke (15:11-32): There the "father" is a symbol and a picture of God, and the "two sons" are symbols and pictures of us, of the humankind. May I ask: Is it clear who really the "lost son" was? Many years ago, during my time as student in Jena we had a guest lecture by Prof. Dr. Eduard Schweizer from Switzerland. He has given a lecture about this important text. And I never forget what I learned on this day: The "lost Son" is not that one, we normally call the "lost Son". The real "lost Son" is that one, who stayed always at home. To him the "father" / God is going and begging – «Отец же его вышед звал его» (стих 28) / "His father came out and entreated him" (verse 28). But this son rejected to follow the father and participate in the festivity with his brother who were away for years. So: In that moment this other son was lost in the eyes of the "father", in the eyes of God!

1.3.2. The special way to express this unique relation from Jesus to God is the term he used for God: "father" – אַבָּא – »Abba«. During the study-time I have learned that this word should be a kind of children's language: "Daddy". But I never believed that really. It's interesting that the parallel word for »Abba« is אִמָּא – »Imma« – "the mother". And then we understand: The Hebrew term for "mother" is אם – »'em«. But »Imma« and »Abba« is not Hebrew. »Abba« is the Aramaic word for "the father". In Hebrew the article is a "he" which we have to put before a word, and in Aramaic the article is an "alaef" which we have to put after a word. "the father" in Hebrew would sound: »hā'ab«, and in Aramaic it sounds »'Abba'«.

1.4. The main challenge is: Christians may realize the privilege they have! They may address God as their "father". Through this word they express their belief that he is the person who is offering them all necessary things, who has created them. When someone has a problematic feeling toward his own parents – then he, then she can believe: I'm created by God, my true and always loving "father" – and "mother", like we learned from Pope John Paul I.

2. My main question: Does lead God into temptation? / Вводит Бог в искушение?

2.1. And now this conviction that someone can call God as his or her "father" has the consequence to reflect about the sixth supplication of the Lord's Prayer: "και μη εισενεγκης ημας εις πειρασμον, αλλα ρυσαι ημας απο του πονηρου" – «И не введи нас в искушение, но избавь нас от лукавого» / "And lead us not into temptation, but deliver us from evil".

There was a discussion going on in the Western Church, especially in the Roman-Catholic Church. I'm asking: What does mean «искушение» / "temptation" really? In my small русско-немецкая словарь from 1929 are given the German terms: "Versuchung" and "Prüfung". When I could translate and understand with "Prüfung" – "to prove" –, no problem would arise. But in the немецко-русская словарь, also from 1929, I find under "Versuchung" only «искушение», but under "Prüfung" I find «проверка» and «испытание» («экзамен» does not matter here) but <u>not</u> the term «искушение»!

And the verb is very important: «вводить» describes a real activity: "to lead into something"! Do we want to speak about God in such a direct way? Therefore, I think my reflection will be important.

2.2. Now it's helpful to look first into a translation of the Lord's Prayer into modern Hebrew.[91] In the sixth supplication we find the term נִסָּיוֹן – "nissajon". It comes from the verb נִסָּה – "nissah", what means: "to prove" – «испытывать». But the dictionary for Biblical Hebrew also gives the meaning "to tempt" – «искушать».[92] What would be correct?

2.2.1. There I have to go back into the past: In the winter semester 1990/91 at the Church Seminary in Leipzig I had to give a lecture on the book of Genesis, the book of Бытие, especially on the stories about the fathers and mothers from Genesis / Бытие 12 on. There I also have lectured the important story about Abraham and his son Isaac in Genesis / Бытие 22. This theologically clearly constructed story starts with the following sentence: וַיְהִי אַחַר הַדְּבָרִים הָאֵלֶּה וְהָאֱלֹהִים נִסָּה אֶת אַבְרָהָם – „Waj‑hi 'achar hadd‑barim ha'ellāh w‑ha'ālohim nissah 'āth 'Abraham". What is said there? In that old time I even did not looked into the German Luther-Bible. Because of theological reasons it was clear for me that there is said: "After these happenings God did prove Abraham." In the English Bible, Revised Standard Version, the same is written: "After these things God tested Abraham." God does not lead into temptation, but God does prove, does test.

2.2.2. One important source for possibilities in the German language is the translation of the Hebrew Bible by the two famous Jewish theologians Martin Buber and Franz Rosenzweig from the Twenties of the last century.[93] I checked all places where we have "nissah" with God as subject – as an activity of God against us[94] – and where we have "nissah" with the human being as subject – as an activity of humankind against God[95] –. In our modern version of the Bible of Martin Luther – „Lutherbibel Revidiert 2017" – we generally have „versuchen" – «искушать». Only in three cases is given „prüfen" – «испытывать».[96] But Martin Buber and Franz Rosenzweig always say „prüfen" or „proben" – «испытывать», never „versuchen" – «искушать»!

---

[91] Cf. „Das Vaterunser. Das Grundgebet der Christenheit in 40 Sprachen", Deutsche Bibelgesellschaft, Stuttgart 2006, p. 39.
[92] See the old dictionary: Wilhelm Gesenius: Handwörterbuch über das Alte Testament, Berlin 1962, p. 507.
I can add: Personally I have an old New Testament in the Hebrew language from London, may be from the 19th century: "Sephär Habb‑rit Hachadāschāh" – "Book of the New Covenant": There in Matthew / Матфея 6:13a is written: לְמַסָּה – "l‑massāh" – "temptation" – «искушение»!
[93] Die Schrift. Verdeutscht von Martin Buber gemeinsam mit Franz Rosenzweig, 10. verbesserte Auflage 1954, Das Buch Im Anfang, p. 57.
[94] Gen 22:1; Ex 15:25; 16:4; 20:20; Deut 8:2.16; 13:4; Judg 2:22; Ps 26:2; 2 Chron 32:31.
[95] Ex 17:2.7; Num 14:22; Deut 6:16; 33,8; Is 7:12; Ps 78:18.41.56; 95:9; 106:14.
[96] Ex 16:4; Judg 2:22; Ps 26:2.

2.2.3. During my stay in Russia in August 2019 I have checked all these biblical places also in the Russian translation, in the Синодальный Перевод. And I've found a very interesting insight: The fathers of this translation of the 19th century have exercised also a typical system. When God is the subject only three times they have written «искушать» / "to tempt", but at the majority of the cases – seven times – they have written: «испытывать» или «испытать» / "to prove"! When we are the subject they had written always «искушать» или «искусить» / "to tempt"! So, these theologians have taught: If someone is bad and tries to guide another one on a wrong way – even God on a wrong way –, then it is we – the humans!

2.2.4. And here I can add an observation from my German language: In this German language the term "versuchen" always has a bad connotation – it's a bad happening, it has a bad actor. Therefore, I think that in German we should never use the term "versuchen" with God as subject, and also not in connection with us in direction to God. I'm very thankful to Martin Buber and Franz Rosenzweig that they never have translated the term "nissah" as "versuchen" – «искушать». There we see again how important it is to listen to our Jewish friends!

2.2.4.1. May I give an example: Under the biblical passages which explain a behavior of humankind in direction to God we have to read Deuteronomy / Второзаконие 6:16a. It was selected in Herrnhut as the Watchword for March 28th, 2019. In the booklet with the Watchwords and Doctrinal texts on that day is written without any content: «Не искушайте Господа, Бога вашего» / "You shall not tempt the Lord your God". By reading this in the morning of that day my really spontaneous reaction was: That's not possible! We cannot tempt God, we cannot lead him to a wrong way, we cannot tempt him in direction of a sin. For us humans that's all is impossible – as long God the Deity is! And for sure Martin Buber and Franz Rosenzweig translated: „Prüfet nicht IHN euern Gott" / "Does not prove the Lord, your God" – and they continued: „wie ihr ihn prüftet bei Prüfe" / "as you tested him at Massah / at the place of prove, and diligently keep the commandments of the Lord, your God!" (verses 16 and 17). This sentence makes the reference to Exodus / Исход 17:1-7, to the story of proving of God by the Israelites where Moses struck the rock that water came out of it. And, what I have to mention: The English translation has here: "You shall not put the Lord your God to the test, as you tested him at Massah" – wonderful! Therefore, I think: This difficult sentence from Deuteronomy / Второзаконие 6:16 you cannot read and meditate without the content. It is bound to this old story. And to attach it to new situations is very dangerous.

But as Doctrinal text for March 28ᵗʰ, 2019 the responsible persons in Herrnhut had added the third supplication of the Lord's Prayer: «Да будет воля Твоя и на земле как на небе!» / "Thy will be done in earth, as it is in heaven!" The idea of these persons in Herrnhut seems to be: In the case a person accepts the will of God within his or her life he or she will not tempt him, will not say: If you do this and that for me then I'm ready to believe you, then I will trust you, then I will offer you a candle and so on. But – might for us as Lutheran Christians such behavior worthwhile? Haven't we reached a fundamentally different behavior? The behavior: "I try to believe" – this means: "I try to understand my life as gift of God and keep this conviction even during difficult periods, even in times of suffering." Could humans try to deal still against such a background with God that he changes his behavior against them? I think we humans never can do this!

2.2.4.2. And into the same direction leads another example – now for God's deeds in direction to us humans: For July 15ᵗʰ, 2019, in Herrnhut the Watchword was selected from Deuteronomy / Второзаконие 13:4: «ибо чрез сие искушает вас Господь, Бог ваш, чтобы узнать, любите ли вы Господа, Бога вашего» / "For the Lord your God is testing you, to know whether you love the Lord your God" [in your Bible and in the English Bible: verse 3!]. But this again is impossible! Because as long God is helping us humans he never leads into temptation – but he proves, he is testing – like it is said in a correct way in the English translation!

2.3. Now I want to draw your attention to a very important statement Apostle Paul had made: In his first letter to the Corinthians he had written in chapter 10: «Вас постигло искушение не иное, как человеческое» / "No temptation has overtaken you that is not common to man" (1 Corinthians / 1-е Коринфянам 10:13a). Here Paul is expressing very clearly that «искушение» / "temptation" does not originates from God or in God, but that «искушение» / "temptation" is always present, and God is active against it, is doing all what he can do to prevent from it. And at this place Paul is continuing: «и верен Бог, Который не попустит вам быть искушаемыми сверх сил» / "God is faithful, and he will not let you be tempted beyond your strength" (verse 13b)!

2.3.1. In the beginning of December in the year 2017 a critique by Pope Francis was published who had criticized the traditional translation of the sixth supplication of the Lord's Prayer.[97] The background was the revision of the biblical texts for the liturgy in France. In December 2017 the new versions have been adopted

---

[97] Cf.: http://de.radiovaticana.va/news/2017/12/06/... (read on December 6ᵗʰ, 2017).

by the Vatican. The sixth supplication traditionally was formulated: „Et ne nous soumets pas à la tentation" – "lead us not into temptation" – «не введи нас в искушение». Now they pray: „Et ne nous laisse pas entrer en tentation" – "let us not fall into temptation" – «не дай нам впасть в искушение» – like Dr. Anton Tichomirow from the seminary in St. Petersburg had taught me!

During the work with this paper in 2019 in the Russian congregations I learned one very important detail by Propst Konstantin Subbotin: There are two contemporary, two modern translations of the New Testament (one of the Russian Bible Society), which offer the following possibilities: «не дай нам поддаться искушению» and «не подвергай нас искушению». When I correctly understand, I would say in German: „Übergib uns nicht der Versuchung", and: „Setze uns nicht der Versuchung aus"; this may mean in English: "Do not transfer us under temptation", and: "Do not expose us to temptation".

2.3.2. After I had given this lecture in Moscow on August 20th, 2019, I could ask the pastor of the French speaking congregation, which gathers in the chapel just near the Lutheran Cathedral, what version they are using. And he answered: "The new one – »Et ne nous laisse pas entrer en tentation« – «не дай нам впасть в искушение»". And in Saransk Reverend Aleksej Stepanowitch Aljoschkin told us in front of his congregation of the "Resurrection", that in the translation of the New Testament into the Mordovian language a formulation is found which expresses precisely that form I was fighting for! But additionally, I learned that the Roman-Catholic Bishops of Russia have made a visit to the Vatican and explained there that the traditional formulation is appropriate for the Russian province of the Roman-Catholic Church: «И не введи нас в искушение» / "And lead us not into temptation."

2.4. But now I want to give two interesting quotes which are in favor of my interpretation:

2.4.1. First the letter of James 1:13-14: «В искушении никто не говори: 'Бог меня искушает': [...] и Сам не искушает никого, Но каждый искушается, увлекаясь и обольщаясь собственною похотью» / "Let no one say when he is tempted: 'I am tempted by God'; [...] and he himself tempts no one; but each person is tempted when he is lured and enticed by his own desire".

2.4.2. Secondly our teacher Martin Luther had written in his Small Catechism: «Хотя Бог и не искушает никого, но мы просим Его [...] охранять и оберегать нас, дабы диавол, мир и плоть наша не смущали нас [...] а также, если мы и подвергнемся таким искушениям, то дать нам в конце концов восторжествоваь»! / „Gott versucht zwar niemand; aber wir bitten in diesem Gebet, daß uns Gott behüte und erhalte, damit uns der Teufel, die Welt und unser Fleisch nicht betrüge [...]; und wenn wir damit angefochten würden, daß wir doch endlich gewinnen"![98] And – what we have to realize – he had quoted our passage of the letter of James!

2.4.3. Therefore I would formulate the following thesis[99]: The Roman-Catholic theologians, Bishops, Cardinals and Pope Francis, who struggled so seriously about the understanding of this crucial sixth supplication of the Lord's Prayer could have just looked into this 490 years old text by our reformer – and all their problems, and all our problems would have been solved!

2.4.4. Again, I'm quoting Pope Francis from the year 2017: "I am the one who is falling. It's not God who is pushing us into temptation to see whether I will be falling. A father does not do this. A father is rushing to help his stumbling child."[100]

From Advent 1st, 2017, on not only in the worship services of the Roman-Catholic Church in France and in Italy but also in the worship services of the Reformed Church and of the Evangelical-Lutheran Church in France the worshippers pray the new, the modified version of the Lord's Prayer, like the French speaking colleague in Moscow said to me in August 2019. A small commentary from March 2018: "Last December God has stopped to set traps for the believers. In her sermon on the 1st of Advent Rev. Agnes von Kirchbach spoke the Lord's Prayer in French language first time in the modified way. [...] Now God does not lead into bad things but he prevents for them."[101]

---

[98] Der Kleine Katechismus D. Martin Luthers / Малый катехизис д-ра Мартина Лютра, Erlangen Third Edition, without a year (but in 2005), p. 18 and 19.
[99] I had formulated this thesis very spontanously in the meeting of the Hungarian pastors in Tarlungeni / Tatrang in Romania on June 12th, 2019 (see note 87).
[100] Papst Franziskus, op. cit. (see note 89), p. 95s (also this translation was made by myself).
[101] Julia Lauer: Mit einer Stimme beten – das geänderte Vaterunser in Frankreich, in: G+H [„Glaube und Heimat" / "Faith and Home Country"] 10, 11.3.2018, p. 14 (also this translation into English was made by myself).

May I end with a personal confession: I'm still praying the Lord's Prayer with the old formulation: „Und führe uns nicht in Versuchung" – «И не введи нас в искушение». But I interpret this supplication against the background of these reflections. And I invite all readers to do this too: God does not tempt us. But it is necessary that we pray to God that he does not prove us! / Он не вводит нас. Но это необходимый молить Бога что Он не испытывать нас!

References

1. „Das Vaterunser. Das Grundgebet der Christenheit in 40 Sprachen", Deutsche Bibelgesellschaft, Stuttgart 2006, p. 39.
2. Der Kleine Katechismus D. Martin Luthers / Малый катехизис д-ра Мартина Лютра, Erlangen Third Edition, without a year (but in 2005), p. 32.
3. Wilhelm Gesenius: Handwörterbuch über das Alte Testament, Berlin 1962, p. 507.
4. https://de.wikipedia.org/Johannes_Paul_I. (read: June 13th, 2020).
5. Julia Lauer: Mit einer Stimme beten – das geänderte Vaterunser in Frankreich, in: G+H [„Glaube und Heimat" / "Faith and Home Country"] 10, 11.3.2018, p. 14.
6. Rainer Neu: „Vatername Gottes, I. Religionsgeschichtlich", Religion in Geschichte und Gegenwart, 4th edition (RGG[4]), vol. 8, 2005, cl. 889.
7. Papst Franziskus: Vaterunser. Das Gebet Jesu neu gelesen, München 2018, p. 18-20.
8. http://de.radiovaticana.va/news/2017/12/06/... (read on December 6th, 2017).

Used books

1. „Das Vaterunser. Das Grundgebet der Christenheit in 40 Sprachen", Deutsche Bibelgesellschaft, Stuttgart 2006, 48 p.
2. Der Kleine Katechismus D. Martin Luthers / Малый катехизис д-ра Мартина Лютра, Erlangen Third Edition, without a year (but in 2005), 32 p.
3. Die Schrift. Verdeutscht von Martin Buber gemeinsam mit Franz Rosenzweig, 10. verbesserte Auflage 1954, Das Buch Im Anfang, 580 p.
4. Wilhelm Gesenius: Handwörterbuch über das Alte Testament, Berlin 1962, 1013 p.
5. „Glaube und Heimat" / "Faith and Home Country"] 10, 11.3.2018, p. 14: Julia Lauer: Mit einer Stimme beten – das geänderte Vaterunser in Frankreich.

6. Langenscheidts Taschenwörterbuch der russischen und deutschen Sprache, Teil I: Russisch-Deutsch, Berlin-Schöneberg ²1929, Teil II: Deutsch-Russisch, Berlin-Schöneberg ³1929.
7. Pope John Paul I.: https://de.wikipedia.org/Johannes_Paul_I. (read: June 13th, 2020).
8. Religion in Geschichte und Gegenwart (RGG), 4th edition, vol. 8, 2005: Rainer Neu: „Vatername Gottes, I. Religionsgeschichtlich", cl. 889-890.
9. "Sephär Habbᵉrit Hachadāschāh" – "Book of the New Covenant", London, without year.
10. The Holy Bible, Revised Standard Version, New York, Glasgow and Toronto 1971
11. Vaterunser. Das Gebet Jesu neu gelesen, by Pope Francis, München 2018, Kösel publishing house, 140 p.

Martin Luther as Translator of the Bible
Мартин Лютер как Переводчик Библии[102]

I.

You may know, that Martin Luther on his way home from Worms, where he stood up for his theses and convictions in front of the Imperial Diet, the „Reichstag", was taken on May 4, 1521 near Eisenach and brought to the Wartburg Castle for refuge, because he had been declared an outlaw. Already four days later, on May 8th, he sent a first letter to his friends in Wittenberg. All contacts were made through Georg Spalatin, the private secretary of the Elector Frederick the Wise. Through these means, it was possible for Luther to receive the books and literature which were necessary for his work. From December 4th to 9th, 1521 it was even possible for him to personally visit in Wittenberg. He stayed secretly in the house of Nikolaus Amsdorf and had several talks with his friends and colleagues. During those days Philipp Melanchthon encouraged him to start with the ambitious plan to translate the Bible.

May I remind you of a very important event: Normally in Eisenach there is a special celebration on May 4th to remember that moment, in which Martin Luther had entered the Wartburg Castle. But on May 4th, 1983 was there a very special event because of the celebration of Luther's 500th birthday. Since September 1982 I could work as assistant to the General Secretary of the Lutheran World Federation, Dr. Carl H. Mau, in Geneva. Together with him I had prepared the sermon he had to give during the Eucharist in the courtyard of the Wartburg Castle. Before this Eucharist was a celebration in the Palace of the Wartburg Castle with a theological paper in its center precisely about the theme of my paper: Dr. Joachim Rogge referred about „Luther als Ausleger der Heiligen Schrift" / "Luther as interpreter of the Holy Scripture".[103] This paper will be the basis of my information. And: You have to imagine: This celebration and also the Eucharist took place under the presence of high ranking politicians of the German Democratic Republic: Horst Sindermann from the Socialist United Party, Gerald

---

[102] This paper was given on 31st of August and on 1st and on 5th of September 2018 in Kazan, in Tscheboksary, and in Syktyvkar and offered for publication on the internet homepage of the Russian newspaper «Proslogion». It is important to reflect about this work which started 500 years ago with the translation of the New Testament!

[103] In: Gott über alle Dinge. Begegnungen mit Martin Luther 1983, Berlin 1984, p.45-57. See there for the first trip to Wittenberg in December 1521: p. 51.

Götting from the Christian Democratic Union and Klaus Gysi, the state secretary for Questions of the Churches!

First Luther decided to start with the translation of the New Testament. For this translation work in 1522 he used several editions of the Greek New Testament – among them the 1519 second edition of the one by Erasmus of Rotterdam (which included a Latin translation). Luther did his translation in only eleven weeks – in a kind of intoxication of work! In September 1522 – shortly before the Leipzig Autumn Fair – the New Testament was published in German, being called therefore the „September Testament".[104]

The translation of the Old Testament, however, required a much longer effort, by Luther along with colleagues. First, we know that, in his time as a monk in Erfurt, Luther bought the book on the Hebrew language, which Johannes Reuchlin had published: "About First Steps in Hebrew".[105] So already in 1522 Luther began the translation of the Torah, of the five Books of Moses. In July 1523 this first part was published in Wittenberg – under the confusing title "The Old Testament German" / „Das Alte Testament Deutsch".

In January 1524 the second part of the Old Testament was published – the books from Joshua to Esther.

But from then on the subsequent books needed longer work. Our Reformation fathers first published the poetical books in October 1524.

In February 1527 the translation of the Book of Isaiah began. Because of the plague, the University moved from Wittenberg to Jena, but Luther remained behind in Wittenberg, without his colleagues. He published the Book of Isaiah in October 1528. In 1530 Daniel was published, then parts of Ezekiel. In 1532 the whole translation of the prophets was published.

At the end of 1532 also was published the Book of Jesus Sirach. And in September 1534 the first edition of the whole Bible was published in Wittenberg and could

---

[104] Petra Schall: 27 Bücher in 70 Tagen. Die Übersetzung des Neuen Testaments auf der Wartburg, in: Dies Buch in aller Zunge, Hand und Herzen. 475 Jahre Lutherbibel, Wartburg-Stiftung Eisenach 2009, pp. 30-42. And cf. Siegfried Raeder: Luther als Ausleger und Übersetzer der Heiligen Schrift, in: H. Junghans (Ed.): Leben und Werk Martin Luthers von 1526 bis 1546, Band I, Berlin ²1985, pp. 253-278, especially p. 272.
[105] „De rudimentis hebraicis".

be sent in time to the Autumn Fair in Leipzig. A huge work – done by Luther, Aquila, Bugenhagen, Cruciger, Melanchthon and others – was completed![106]

II.

First, we have to recognize that <u>Luther was a scholar</u>. His normal language was Latin. And – for sure – the most important works he had written to date were in Latin. This means: that he thought in that language. For example, his famous 95 Theses of autumn 1517 about indulgences were written and published in Latin. Only later were they translated into the German language.[107]

In May and June of this year 2018, I spent five weeks in Braşov / Kronstadt / Brassó in Romania, serving in the German-speaking Lutheran congregation there. The reformer of that town and region was Johannes Honterus. In 1543, he published his "Booklet on Reformation". But he published it in Latin: "Reformatio Ecclesiae Coronensis ac totius Barcensis Provinciae" – "The Reformation of the Church of Kronstadt and of the whole Burzen Area".[108] When he read it in front of the members of the council of his town – it was, naturally, in Latin! In those days, all leaders of the town have understood Latin.

But <u>Luther also was a preacher</u>. He was used to preaching on biblical texts – in German language. But in which German language did he do it? Luther's

---

[106] Cf. Siegfried Raeder, op. cit. (note 104) pp. 253-278, esp. pp. 256.270-274. Cf. Jutta Krauß: Werdegang in Wittenberg. Die Übersetzung des Alten Testaments, in: Dies Buch in aller Zunge, Hand und Herzen (note 104), pp. 43-49, and Hilmar Schwarz: Luthers Bibelkollegium, in the same publication, pp. 50-54.

[107] Here I want to give an additional information: In both universities where I could give this paper, in Tscheboksary and in Syktyvkar, I had the impression that for the majority of the students Reformation and Lutheranism were new. Therefore, I informed that in the 17th century the decision was made to use the date of publication of the 95 Theses to celebrate the Reformation. This means that we do this since then on October 31st. In 2017 we could celebrate the 500. anniversary of Reformation – all over the world, also in Russia. There the two Lutheran Churches have done this: the Evangelical Lutheran Church in Russia and the Evangelical Lutheran Church of Ingria in Russia. One most important event was the transferring of the Cathedral of St. Peter and St. Paul in Moscow into the ownership of the congregation and the church. At this celebration on October 25th, 2017, also the President of the Federal Republic of Germany, Frank-Walter Steinmeier, and the Chairman of the EKD Council, Bishop Heinrich Bedford-Strohm, Munich, attended (cf.: «Историческая справедливость восстанавливается». Кафедральный собор в Москве передан в собственность, в Лютеранские Вести, № 11 (207), Ноябрь 2017, pp, 1-2. See also: „Steinmeier bei Rückgabe der Kathedrale ‚St. Peter und Paul' in Moskau an Lutheraner", in: https://de.sputniknews.com/gesellschaft/20171025318030611-steinmeier-bei-rückgabe... (25.10.2017). During the lectures I expressed my sincere thanks to the Russian government for the decision to give the church building to the church.

[108] Cf. B. Heigl and Th. Şindilariu (Ed.): Johannes Honterus. Reformatio ecclesiae Coronensis ac totius Barcensis provinciae. Corona 1543, Quellen zur Geschichte der Stadt Kronstadt, Band VIII, Beiheft 2, Kronstadt 2017.

childhood language was the Saxon dialect spoken in Mansfeld, where he grew up. And he was familiar with the official language in the Saxon Duchy. One time he said in his table talks: "I don't have a specific language in German, but I use the normal German language, so that both – the southern and the northern Germans – do understand me. I speak according to the Saxon administration. All dukes and kings in Germany, all towns of the Empire, all courts and administrations are following this praxis. Therefore, it is the common German language."[109]

From this basis he could develop this common German language, which was understood in most German areas – that's the first aspect. And the second aspect is that this, his German, was successful with time and practice, because people used it to read and listen to the texts from Luther. And therefore, this German was becoming the common German language!

But additionally, he had the challenge to find the appropriate wordings and formulations for all things. Therefore, he was always learning. For example, he went to the butcher, looked at his work, and asked for the terms he used. He explained: "It is necessary, to ask the mother in the house, the children in the street, and the normal man in the market place, and do look at their mouths, how they speak, and then translate according to that practice. Then they understand, and they realize that we do speak with them in German."[110]

We can summarize: His hard work, his gifts, his poetical ability and his theological and spiritual consciousness helped him very much: "because God has opened my mouth and has ordered me to speak [...]"[111] – as he expressed it once. "I was keen in translating. My aim was to speak a clean and clear German. Therefore,

---

[109] Birgit Stolt: Luthers Übersetzungstheorie und Übersetzungspraxis, in: H. Junghans (Ed.) (note 104), p. 250: „Ich habe keine gewisse, sonderliche, eigene Sprache im Deutschen, sondern brauche der gemeinen deutschen Sprache, daß mich beide, Ober- und Niederländer, verstehen mögen. Ich rede nach der sächsischen Canzeley, welcher nachfolgen alle Fürsten und Könige in Deutschland, alle Reichsstädte, Fürsten-Höfe [...], darum ist's auch die gemeinste deutsche Sprache." (The English version in the text I translated from the German original.) Cf. Martin Luther, WA TR 2, p. 639. Cf. then: Joachim Rogge, op. cit. (note 103), p. 53.

[110] Petra Schall, op. cit. (note 104), pp. 39-40: „[...] sondern man muss die Mutter im Haus, die Kinder auf der Gasse, den gemeinen Mann auf dem Markt drum fragen, und denselbigen auf das Maul sehen, wie sie reden, und danach dolmetschen. So verstehen sie es denn und merken, dass man Deutsch mit ihnen redet." Cf. Martin Luther, WA 30, II, p. 637 (his "Letter on Translating" / „Sendbrief vom Dolmetschen" from 1530).

[111] Jutta Krauß: Luthers Sprache. Wartburgland und Wittenberg als Wiege des Neuhochdeutschen, in: Dies Buch in aller Zunge, Hand und Herzen (note 104), p. 74: „[...] weil mir Gott den Mund aufgetan hat und heissen reden [...]." (The English version in the text I translated from the German original.) The same: Wackersteine und Klötze. Luthers Dolmetschen, in the same publication (note 103), pp. 76-84.

often we had to ask for the precise wording for fourteen days, for three or four weeks – and even then have not really found it."[112]

May I conclude this part with an example: In a meditation during the Advent Season in 2010 I looked at Mary, the mother of Jesus. In the Roman Catholic Church there is a common prayer: "Hail, Mary, full of grace. The Lord is with you." The beginning of this prayer comes from Luke 1:28 and has to be considered carefully. Here we can learn much from Martin Luther:

In 1520-21 he translated and interpreted the Song of Mary, the "Magnificat", which we find in Luke 1. There he wrote: "The opinion of Mary is as follows: God has looked at me as a poor, despised and unsightly girl. But he could have found daughters of rich, noble and powerful kings and lords. [...] But he has looked at me and used a low and disdained maidservant that no one praises before him, that he would be worthy. [...] And therefore she does not praise her worthiness or unworthiness, but only the fact that God has looked at her [...]."[113]

And therefore in 1522 Luther was reflecting at Wartburg Castle about what would be the appropriate translation. His formulation: "Greetings to you, gracious one, the Lord is with you." Here Mary is addressed not because of her own abilities but because of the gifts which she had received from God. At another place Luther even suggested the following wording: "God is greeting you, dear Mary."[114]

Now I would like to consider two Bible translations. In the Revised Standard Version we read: "Hail, O favoured one, the Lord is with you!" Here Mary is understood as one who has received "favour" by God. And your Библия reads: "Радуйся, благодатная!" This Russian term – and I hope that I understand it

---

[112] Birgit Stolt, op. cit. (note 109), p. 245: „Ich habe mich dessen geflissen im Dolmetschen, dass ich rein und klar Deutsch geben möchte. Und ist uns wohl oft begegnet, dass wir vierzehn Tage, drei, vier Wochen haben ein einzelnes Wort gesucht und gefragt, haben es dennoch zuweilen nicht gefunden." (The English version in the text I translated from the German original.) Cf. Martin Luther, WA 30, II, p. 636.

[113] Cf. Rainer Stahl, Wer ist die Wahrheit? Biblische Predigten zu Themen unserer Zeit, Bau Bassin 2018, pp. 5-6: „Gott hat auf mich armes, verachtetes, unansehnliches Mädchen gesehen und hätte wohl Töchter von reichen, hohen, edlen, mächtigen Königen, Fürsten und großen Herren finden können. [...] Aber er hat auf mich seine reinen, gütigen Augen geworfen und so eine geringe, verschmähte Magd dazu gebraucht, damit sich niemand vor ihm rühme, dass er würdig gewesen wäre [...]. Und darum rühmt sie nicht ihre Würdigkeit noch ihre Unwürdigkeit, sondern allein dessen, dass Gott sie angesehen hat." (The English version in the text I translated from the German original.) Cf. Martin Luther, Magnificat.

[114] Siegfried Raeder, op. cit. (note 104), p. 275: „Gott grüße dich, du liebe Maria [...]." (The English version in the text I translated from the German original.) Cf. Martin Luther, WA 30, II, p. 638.

correctly – connects both possibilities: Mary is understood as one who is blessed by God. But Mary is also understood as one who gives blessings to others.

Martin Luther would prefer only the first understanding: Mary is important for us because she is blessed by God. And as a blessed one she becomes a model for us. We as well should be ready to receive the blessing of God and give this blessing a structure in the reality of our lives. She is a model for us, she has gone along a way in which we can follow her. Like Mary, we can also be ready to receive gifts from God.

III.

In this part I would like to look at <u>Martin Luther as exegete, as theologian</u>. All his translation work can only be understood by recognizing this important fact. As we know, Luther was expert in Bible exegesis. In his time as professor in Wittenberg he gave lectures on biblical books. This was his academic work.

He started from 1513 to 1515 with a lecture on the Book of Psalms. (As I was starting my academic career at the Theological Seminary in Leipzig, I had to give a lecture in the spring 1989 on the Book of Psalms, and I mentioned that this would be a wonderful parallel to Luther!) From 1515 to 1516 Luther gave a lecture about the letter to the Romans, then until spring 1517 about the letter to the Galatians, and until spring 1518 about the letter to the Hebrews. From 1519 to 1521 he lectured again on the Psalms. In 1523-1524 he interpreted the Book of Deuteronomy, from 1524 to 1526 the Book of the Small Prophets. And so on. The lecture with which he finished his work, from 1535 to 1545, was on the Book of Genesis.[115]

Luther always worked with the Latin Bible, as well as with the Greek and Hebrew Bibles. In the famous exhibition "Luther!" in 2017 in Wittenberg we could see the Hebrew Bible Luther owned. This Bible was printed in the year 1494 in Brescia; he received it between 1515 and 1519, and he used it until the end of his life.

In this connection we may emphasize a very important principle of interpreting the Bible: Luther recognized <u>that Jesus Christ is its center</u>. We as Christians and also all others must read the Bible in the light of Christ. He developed a very

---

[115] Siegfried Raeder, op. cit. (note 104), pp. 255-257, and also Joachim Rogge, op. cit. (note 104), p. 49.

important formulation: To identify whether the books of the Bible „Christum treiben oder nicht"[116] = whether they relate to Christ and lead us to Christ or not. I think we have to understand that formulation in a complex way. In my lecture in spring 1989 I mentioned in opposition to Luther, that it is not important whether the Psalms speak directly about Jesus Christ, but that it is important to realize that we can understand them from our knowledge and faith in Christ. "Because of that, Luther was looking for the proclamation of the Messiah and therefore for the »Gospel« in the Hebrew Bible and found it there. Therefore, the Hebrew Bible as Old Testament was for him the treasure of the Christian Church. But it should be read by starting with Christ and by coming to Christ. Then it would open to us – as he was convinced – its full truth."[117] Or in the words of Joachim Rogge: "The Justice of God is his mercy"[118] – and only when we have understood this we are able to understand the message of the Bible.

The next important distinction, which Martin Luther recognized and defended during his lifetime, is the distinction between Law and Gospel. He was convinced that only those are good theologians, who are able to discern Law and Gospel. This means: to keep them together and to distinguish them: "Nearly the whole Holy Scripture and the knowledge of the whole theology are dependent on the correct knowledge of Law and Gospel."[119] The word of God as Law remains important, but not as a way to salvation, rather as a mirror which shows us that we need the Gospel which frees us and enables us to live in a new way.

And now we come to the third distinction which is especially important for the translation work: the distinction between letter and spirit. Martin Luther constantly struggled with this important challenge. To recognize the letter in a correct way is the basis, but to understand the meaning, the spirit, which is expressed by the wording of the biblical text, is the aim of all the work. He said: "Therefore I

---

[116] Hans-Martin Barth: Hermeneutisches Erbe der Reformation und interreligiöser Dialog, in: LUTHER 89, 2018, p. 48. Cf. Martin Luther, WA DB 7, p. 384.
[117] Johannes Schilling: Martin Luthers Handexemplar einer Hebräischen Bibel, in: Luther! 95 Schätze – 95 Menschen, Stiftung Luthergedenkstätten in Sachsen-Anhalt 2017, p. 110: „Denn in der hebräischen Bibel suchte und fand Luther die Verkündigung des Messias und damit das »Evangelium«. Deshalb war ihm die hebräische Bibel als Altes Testament ein unaufgebbarer Schatz der christlichen Kirche. Aber sie sollte eben von Christus her und auf ihn hin gelesen werden, um, wie er überzeugt war, ihre Wahrheit voll zu erschließen [...]". (The English version in the text I translated from the German original.)
[118] Joachim Rogge, op. cit. (note 104), p. 50.
[119] Hans Martin Barth, op. cit. (note 116), p. 47. (The English version in the text I translated from the German original.) Cf. Martin Luther, WA 7, p. 502.

have to give up the letters, and have to search how the German man speaks",[120] and have to ask what the spirit of God is telling us through a given biblical formulation.

I would like to summarize this part of my paper: Our Lutheran Christianity is in a way complicated. We do not have easy answers with which we can deal with all questions of our life. But our Lutheran Christianity offers us distinctions we can use to find our own answers to the question of how to live as Christians. An important one is that of <u>the distinction of the Two Kingdoms</u>, the distinction between the work of God by his right hand and the work of God by his left hand. May be this is one reason that we are often a small group, that huge masses do not follow us, but rather our people are those who have learned to live with these distinctions. In a seminar of the Martin-Luther-Bund in 2002 Günther Gassmann, in the beginning of the Eighties theologian in the Studies Department of the Lutheran World Federation and later director of the department "Faith and Order" in the World Council of Churches, gave a similar explanation about the "Fundamentals of the Lutheran Identity".[121] It is very important not to forget this but to deal with it daily.

May I conclude this part of my paper also with a concrete example: In a sermon on Reformation Day in 2010 in Havířov-Bludovice in the Czech Republic I discussed the translation of Romans 3:28 by Luther.[122] And again on Reformation Day in 2016 in Möhrendorf near Erlangen I discussed this problem.[123] I suggested that we can follow the following steps:

In April 1518 Martin Luther presented his insights in Heidelberg during a theological meeting of the community of the monasteries of his order (the "Augustinians", die „Augustiner Eremiten"). There he said in thesis 25: "Not that one, who makes much, is justified, but that one, who believes much in Christ without deeds." And he gave the following argument: "Because the justification by God [...] will be implemented through faith. [...] Therefore I will understand this 'without deeds' in the following way: Not that the justified do nothing, but that his

---

[120] Birgit Stolt, op. cit. (note 109), p. 245: „Darum muss ich hie die Buchstaben fahren lassen und forschen, wie der Deutsche Mann solches redet." (The English version in the text I translated from the German original.) Cf. WA 30 II, p. 639.
[121] Günther Gassmann: Grundelemente lutherischer Identität als verbindendes und verpflichtendes Band weltweiter lutherischer Gemeinschaft, in: Lutherische Kirche in der Welt, Jahrbuch des Martin-Luther-Bundes, Folge 50, 2003, pp. 23-35. (The English version in the text I translated from the German original.)
[122] Rainer Stahl: Predigten für die Diaspora. Durch das Kirchenjahr zu Gast in Gemeinden von Minderheitskirchen, Saarbrücken 2014, pp. 215-219.
[123] Rainer Stahl, op. cit. (note 113), pp. 212-216.

deeds do not create his justification, but instead that his justification creates his deeds." And then he quoted Romans 3:28: "For we hold that a man is justified by faith apart from works of law."[124] To understand this formulation we have to keep in mind that Luther delivered his theses and the explanations in Heidelberg in Latin, so he quoted the Vulgata, the Latin Bible.

But in 1522 at the Wartburg Castle, as Martin Luther translated the New Testament into German, he wrote: "For we hold that a man is justified apart from works of law by faith <u>alone</u>." This addition of "alone" provoked much critique. Therefore in 1530 he defended himself and wrote: "What's going on, that they rage and burn? The problem is very clear and shows that faith alone is able to grasp the death and resurrection of Christ without any deeds, and that his death and resurrection is our life and justification."[125]

It's interesting to see how Bibles in other languages have this sentence: In 2010 I found that the Czech Bible: "[...], že se člověk stává spravedlivým vírou bez skutků zákona" – is without "alone". The Revised Standard Version reads as we heard it already: "[...], that a man is justified by faith apart from works of law" – without "alone". And your Bible reads: "[...] что человек оправдывается верую, независимо от дел закона" – again without "alone" / без «только»! In February 2019 I learned from the Hungarian Lutheran colleague Tibor Missura that in the first edition of the New Testament, made by the Lutheran theologian János Szilveszter (1504-1551) in 1541, Romans 3:28 was without "alone". But in June 2018 Péter Szeghljánik, a Reformed Hungarian colleague from the Western Ukraine in Béregszász / Beregowo, had informed me that the Hungarian Bible from 1589, translated by the Reformed theologian Gáspár Károlyi (1529-1592) from Transylvania, had this additional "alone". Presently the Hungarian Bible does not have this "alone" any more. Also very interesting is the situation in the Slovenian Bible: Juri Dalmatin used in his translation from 1584 the "alone": "satu my tèrdnu dèrshimo, de Zhlovik pravizhen poſtane, pres del te Poſtave, **le ſkuſi vero**." But

---

[124] Martin Luther: Disputatio Heidelbergae Habita 1518 / Heidelberger Disputation 1518, in: Lateinisch-Deutsche Studienausgabe, Bd. 1, Leipzig 2006, pp. 57-59: „Nicht der ist gerecht, der viel wirkt, sondern der ohne Werk viel an Christus glaubt." „Denn die Gerechtigkeit wird [...] eingegossen durch den Glauben. [...] Von daher will ich jenes (»ohne Werk«) so verstanden wissen: nicht, dass der Gerechte nichts wirke, sondern dass seine Werke nicht seine Gerechtigkeit bewirken, sondern vielmehr seine Gerechtigkeit die Werke bewirkt." (The English version in the text I translated from the German original.)

[125] Siegfried Raeder, op. cit. (note 104), p. 276. „Was ist's denn nun, dass man so tobet und wütet, ketzert und brennt, so die Sache doch im Grund klar daliegt und beweist, dass allein der Glaube Christi Tod und Auferstehung fasse ohne alle Werke, und derselbige Tod und Auferstehung unser Leben und unsere Gerechtigkeit sei." Cf. Martin Luther, WA 30, II, p. 642.

the reformer of Slovenia, Primos Trubar, had followed Erasmus of Rotterdam and not used the "alone": "Satu mi terdnu dershimo, De ta zhlouik bode Prauizhin fturien skufi to Vero, pres tih del te Poftaue." And also the modern Bible in Slovenia of 2008 has not the "alone" – as Rev. Aleksander Erniša, a slovenian colleague from Triest, had written to me on March 20th, 2019.

By adding this word "alone" Martin Luther sharpened the position of St. Paul: Before God we are only persons who receive. Before God we cannot mention anything against our own ability or against our own power or against our own success. There we are always donee.[126]

IV.

Now I would like to discuss one important example. In this discussion the translation by Martin Luther will be only one of various solutions to the problems – and not the best one.[127]

For a long time, I have difficulties with the traditional translation of Genesis 1:26,27. What are the Hebrew sentences really saying?

[...] ויאמר אלהים נעשה אדם בצלמנו כדמותנו וירדו בדגת הים
ויברא אלהים את האדם בצלמו בצלם אלהים ברא אתו

= "Wajjo'mär 'Älohim na'asäh 'Adam b^ezalmenu kidmuthenu. W^ejirdu bidgath Hajjam [...]
Wajjibra' 'Älohim 'äth Ha'Adam b^ezalmo, b^ezäläm 'Älohim bara' 'otho".

In the spring of 1991 in Leipzig in preparing my lecture about the first part of the Book of Genesis, I learned from an article by Manfred Görg, Munich, that the original meanings of these terms are seen in the old Egyptian language and also in Genesis in chapter 5:1,3: The son is the new manifestation of the father, therefore he is capable of doing what the father was able to do: "He [Adam] begat a son in his likeness, after his image" (Genesis 5:3). And from there we understand the sentence: "When God created humankind, he made it in the likeness of God" (Genesis 5:1). This means: Humankind does not look like God. That's impossible. Therefore, humankind is not the image, not the picture of God, which is often

---

[126] Cf. also Joachim Rogge, op. cit. (note 103), p. 54.
[127] For this publication I have to underline that I have not read that part of my paper because I had the impression that it would be too difficult for a first listening. But I think for reading and reflection it might be of interest.

said. But humankind is – as I like to say – the representative of God on earth with a special task: to govern the animals. In this task with regard to the animals we see the quality of humankind – by the way: common for male and female, because the Hebrew sentence ends: זכר ונקבה = "zakar unqebah" = "male and female".

Therefore, I translate our Hebrew passage this way: "Then God said: Let us make humankind as our representative and with our qualification / with our quality to govern upon the fishes of the water [...]. So, God created humankind as his representative, as representative of God he created it" (Genesis 1:26,27).

Already in 2000 Bernd Janowski published in the fourth edition of the famous dictionary "Religion in Past and Present" („Religion in Geschichte und Gegenwart") a short article about the "Imago Dei" („Gottebenbildlichkeit"), from which I want to quote the central information in a free translation into English: Genesis 1:26 contains three related statements – concerning the creation, concerning the image, and concerning the governing. First it explains the assertion that humankind does represent God with respect to the earth, secondly it explains the aspect of image, with which the understanding of an identity between humankind and God should be avoided, and thirdly it explains the aspect of government of humankind over the earth and the animals.[128]

I have the feeling that the translation of our sentences into the Greek language bridges to the Christian doctrine of "Imago Dei": The Jews in the third century before Christ in Egypt translated: "κατ' εικονα ημετεραν" – "concerning our image" and „ καθ' ομοιωσιν" – "concerning likeness" (Genesis 1:26). First, we have to recognize, that "in the understanding of the Septuagint humankind was not created in similarity to God but in similarity to the imagination of God – to the picture about humankind God had in mind"![129] And secondly, I have the feeling, that the second phrase – "concerning likeness" – provoked the misunderstanding, that humankind was created in a special way to be like God.

---

[128] Bernd Janowski: Art. Gottebenbildlichkeit, I. Altes Testament und Judentum, in: RGG⁴, Band 3, 2000, 1159-1160: „[...] daß Gen 1,26-31 drei aufeinander bezogene Aussagen (Schöpfungs-, Bild- und Herrschaftsaussage) enthält. [...] den funktionalen Aspekt der G.[ottebenbildlichkeit] im Sinne des *Repräsentationsgedankens* betont, [...] um eine Identität von Bild (Mensch) und Abgebildetem (Gott) zu vermeiden, diesen Aspekt im Sinn einer *Vergleichbarkeit* des Menschen mit Gott. [...] Worin sich die G.[ottebenbildlichkeit] erweist, sagt in Gen 1,26 der an die Bildbegriffe anschließende Finalsatz: »damit sie (sc. die Menschen) herrschen über die Fische des Meeres [...]«."

[129] P. Prestel u. S. Schorch: Genesis / Das erste Buch Mose, in: Septuaginta Deutsch. Erläuterungen und Kommentare I, Stuttgart 2011, p. 159. (The English version in the text I translated from the German original.)

Therefore, I am a convinced friend of the purely orthodox painting tradition, in which there is no picture of God possible, except the picture of Jesus Christ. Therefore, the image of God is the image of Christ – for example in the dome of the cupola of a church. This I had seen again this year in the Church of the "Saviour on the Blood" in St. Petersburg:[130]

(The photo was taken on March 1st, 2018.)

V. Attachment[131]

What I did not yet mention in detail is the fact that Martin Luther created many formulations which have since become idiomatic sentences and phrases in German.[132] I only want to draw your attention to this fact – which is very important –, because it's very difficult for me to show and demonstrate this in another language than German. But one example I want to give you:

Matthew 12:34 (Luke 6:41):

a) In Greek the sentence sounds: "εκ γαρ του περισσευματος της καρδιας το στομα λαλει."
b) The Revised Standard Version (1952)[133] has translated it as: "For out of the abundance of the heart the mouth speaks."
c) Your Russian Bible (1873) reads: «Ибо от избытка сердца говорят уста.»

---

[130] Cf. Georgy Butikov: The Church of the Saviour on the Blood, Saint Petersburg (see also above: "Christian Belief for Today", 4.1.).
[131] Even this part never was read in front of the different audiences, it would be important for reading to grasp this very famous aspect of Luther's work for the German language.
[132] See also: Joachim Rogge, op. cit. (note 103), p. 53-54.
[133] The Holy Bible. Revised Standard Version, Bible Society, Old Testament from 1952, New Testament form 1971.

d) Klaus Berger (2001)[134] had translated: „Denn der Mund verrät, wovon das Herz übervoll ist."

e) Luise Schottroff, has formulated in the „Bibel in gerechter Sprache" / „Bible in the Language of Justice" (2006)[135]: „Denn wovon das Herz überfließt, davon spricht der Mund."

f) The Zürcher Bibel (2006)[136] says: „Spricht doch der Mund nur aus, wovon das Herz überquillt."

g) But Luther had formulated (in the edition from 1903, which I had received as gift to my confirmation in 1965): „Wes das Herz voll ist, des gehet der Mund über."

The most modern edition: Lutherbibel (revidiert 2017): „Wes das Herz voll ist, des geht der Mund über."

This I would translate into English: "About what the heart is full, this overflows from the mouth."

And into Russian, I think: «Ибо от сердца полна, уста перегаёт.»

Many thanks! Большое Спасибо![137]

---

[134] Klaus Berger und Christiane Nord: Das Neue Testament und frühchristliche Schriften, Frankfurt / Main und Leipzig, 5. Auflage, 2001.
[135] Bibel in *gerechter* Sprache, Gütersloh 2006.
[136] Zürcher Bibel 2007, Zürich 2007.
[137] For the improvement of the English, I am very thankful to Ralston Deffenbaugh, Geneva, former Assisting General Secretary of the Lutheran World Federation.

Martin Luther as Poet of Hymns[138]

I.

In the beginning we have to understand that Martin Luther has received a special education in music – to play an instrument, to sing and to compose melodies. In the schools in Mansfeld, Magdeburg and Eisenach it was practice to start and to end the school hours by singing. One important step was his participation in a group of school boys singing in Eisenach to receive money or just bread from the people. Later he has called himself: „Partekenhengst". How this word could be translated? It's speaking of a serving horse, this means: of a boy who is going around to beg for bread – by singing together with friends.[139] In his time in Eisenach the widow Mrs. Cotta has invited him to her house. Until now a house not far from the town church is shown as the house of Mrs. Cotta which is now the "Luther-House" in Eisenach. But during my stay and work in Eisenach from 1992 to 1998 I have understood that the original house of Mrs. Cotta maybe was on a different place in the town. This might be a question, which would be of interest for persons, who are interested in historical details. For us the following is important: From the very beginning education in music was important for Martin Luther, then also in the time as a student in Erfurt and for sure in the time as a monk there. His musicality was very much developed!

Then one very important step for him to become a poet was very crucial. To understand that step it is necessary to mention his first important publications. Here I refer to an edition of works of Martin Luther in five volume which was published in the GDR and where my teacher of systematic theology, Prof. Dr. Horst Beintker, also had worked:[140]

> First: in October / November 1517 his "95 Theses on Indulgence", several times printed until the end of 1517 (Nuremberg, Leipzig, Basel),
> secondly: in March 1518 his very important "Sermon on Indulgence and Grace",
> thirdly: in June 1520 his "Sermon on the Good Deeds",

---

[138] This paper was prepared for Чебоксары, Russia, 2020, but so far it could not be given (March 2022). But the German version was published in the yearbook of the Martin-Luther-Bund: Lutherische Kirche in der Welt. Jahrbuch des Martin-Luther-Bundes, Folge 68, 2021, p. 63-93.
[139] Cf. Martin Rößler: Martin Luther, in: Martin Rößler: Liedermacher im Gesangbuch. Liedgeschichte in Lebensbildern, Stuttgart 2001, p. 36.
[140] Cf. Martin Luther Taschenausgabe, Auswahl in fünf Bänden, ed. by Horst Beintker, Helmar Junghans and Hubert Kirchner, Berlin 1981-1984.

fourthly: in August 1520 already in two editions with each one of 4.000 copies his publication on the reform of Christianity, addressed to the "Christian Nobility of the German Nation",

fifth: in the beginning of October 1520 his book about the "De captivitate Babylonica ecclesiae", "Babylonian Imprisonment of the Church"[141],

and sixth: in the beginning of November of that year his book on the "Liberty of a Christian Person", which he also had sent to Pope Leo X. in a Latin translation.[142]

Imagine all these totally new ideas and argumentations in only two and a half years!

Because of all of that a trial of the church against him started in June 1520 with the Papal letter about the possible excommunication of him, the bull which describes the possible Ban, and in the beginning of January 1521 the letter with his excommunication, the Ban bull, by the Pope. And in April 1521 Luther had to defend his positions in front of the Imperial Diet in Worms and was on May 4th, 1521, taken to refuge in the Wartburg Castle near Eisenach.

Many people have read his publications. His thoughts went a way of triumph through whole Germany and through many countries of Europe. Therefore, on July 1st, 1523, two colleagues of the order of the "Augustinian Eremites", to which Martin Luther himself belonged, in Belgium, in Brussels, have been sentenced to death and burnt – Heinrich Voss / Heinrich Voes and Johannes van den Esschen / Johann van Esch.[143] The information about this murder – I really say "murder"! – resulted for Martin Luther in a deep trauma: Others have been ready to suffer and even to die for the theological insights he had won! Then he wrote already in the year 1523 a hymn about them – and by this he wrote his first poem.[144] To give you an impression of this important hymn I want to try to translate some lines from the verses 1, 2 and 12 from the German original[145] into English. Additional

---

[141] Cf. Martin Luther, Lateinisch-deutsche Studienausgabe, Vol. 3, ed. by Günther Wartenberg (+) and Michael Beyer, Leipzig 2009.
[142] See the working books: Befreit! Martin Luthers Hauptschriften von 1520, ed. in the name of the United Evangelical Lutheran Church in Germany by Heiko Franke and Georg Raatz, Vol. 1: Theologische Einführungen und Themeneinheiten, especially p. 16.22, Vol. 2: Textauszüge und Anregungen, especially p. 12.14, Leipzig 2020.
[143] Cf. Martin Rößler, op. cit. (see note 139), p. 38. And see: Konrad Klek: „Singen und Sagen". Reformatorisches Singen als öffentlicher Protest, in: Peter Bubmann und Konrad Klek (Hg.): Davon ich singen und sagen will. Die Evangelischen und ihre Lieder, Leipzig 2012, p. 11-26.
[144] Cf. Martin Rößler, op. cit. (see note 139), p. 38-39. Also cf. Dick Akerboom: „Ein neues Lied wir heben an", in: Lutherische Kirche in der Welt, Jahrbuch des Martin-Luther-Bundes, Folge 55, 2008, p. 63-82.
[145] Cf.: Rainer Stahl: Martin Luther für uns heute, Erlangen 2008, p. 39-40.

I can quote a translation into Russian by L. N. Nazarenko / Л. Н. Назаренко,[146] which seems to be relatively free:

„Ein neues Lied wir heben an,   "A new hymn we start,
des walt Gott, unser Herre,   which God, our Lord, may help us.
zu singen, was Gott hat getan   To sing what God had done
zu seinem Lob und Ehre   for his praise and honor.
Zu Brüssel in dem Niederland   In Brussels in the Netherlands
wohl durch zwei junge Knaben   through two young boys
hat er seine Wundermacht bekannt […]   he had given known his miracles […]

«Мы песню новую начнем, –
С благословенья Божия.
Что совершил Он, воспоем,
Дела благие множа.
В Брюсселе, в Нидерландах, – там
Двух юношей избрал Он,
[…] явить всем нам
Чудесной власти право […]

[…] Von dieser Welt geschieden sind,   […] From this world they have passed away.
sie haben die Kronen erworben.   They have received their crowns
Recht wie die frommen Gotteskinder   like the pious children of God.
für sein / ihr Wort sind sie gestorben […].   They died for his / their word […].

[…] Они покинули сей мир,
Снискав венец терновый.
Шли, дети Божии, на смерть –
В огонь – за Его Слово,
Ученики Христовы.

[…] Wir sollen danken Gott darin,   […] We should thank God because of this.
sein Wort ist wiederkommen.   His word has come back again.
Der Sommer ist hart vor der Tür,   The summer is just in front of the door.
der Winter ist vergangen […].   The winter has gone already […].
Der das hat angefangen,   Who has started all of this
der wird es wohl vollenden."   will bring it to the fulfillment."

[…] Должны мы Господа хвалить:
Вновь с нами Слово Божье!

---

[146] Cf. Генрих Фаусель: Мартин Лютер, Жизнь и дело, Том 2, 1522–1546, Перевод с немецкого Ю. А. Голубкина, Харьков 1996, стр. 75-77.

> Стучится лето в двери к нам,
> Утихли рек разливы
> Нежна цветов голубизна:
> Кто начал все красиво, –
> Тот завершит на диво!»

Of special interest is the Russian version in verse 12: Martin Luther was speaking about the fact that the winter had come to an end and the summer is near. The translator into Russian had chosen the picture that the floods of rivers have become quiet, what means, that the spring has come to an end, and he has chosen the picture of blue flowers: «Утихли рек разливы / Нежна цветов голубизна».

Here the poetry and the music are showing their power – like Martin Luther intended. The Professor for Church Music in Erlangen, Konrad Klek, had written: "»*To sing and to say*« – this common word [...] is the formula for mass communication in times without newspapers, radio and internet. What singers are giving in the public of streets and market places are heard by many, also are sung and repeated."[147] This hymn went from mouth to mouth and showed how this terrible happening could be overcome by the help of music.

In a general way Konrad Klek had underlined: "Often representatives of the Roman church have shown that the hymns have become the best weapons for the Protestants. In Hildesheim, the town of a bishop, already in 1524 and then again in 1531 it was forbidden to sing openly hymns of the reformation. Because of that the people went out of the town together with their hymns. Even in private rooms it was not possible to sing without punishment. In Brunswick in the year 1526 youngsters have been reported to the priest."[148]

In those years it became a typical power to proclaim the insights of the Gospel: People have become ambassadors of this newly discovered Gospel – by singing the hymns which Martin Luther had created! All of this shows how important these hymns have been.

---

[147] Konrad Klek, op. cit. (see note 143), p. 13 (the translation into English is by myself).
[148] Konrad Klek, op. cit. (see note 143), p. 24 (the translation into English is by myself).

II.

Now I want to quote three hymns from which Luther had written the texts and also the melodies. I'm inviting you to sing these hymns according to his melodies! I'm happy that I can use a description of your Ingrian Church, I had given six years ago, and within I also compared the hymn books of your church and of the Evangelical-Lutheran Church of Russia.[149]

II.1.

From the end of 1523 and the beginning of 1524 the following hymn is important: „Aus tiefer Not schrei ich zu dir". In our German hymn Book it has the hymn number 299[150], in "Laudamus", the hymnal for the Lutheran World Federation[151], the hymn number 98 and in the "Lutheran Book of Worship"[152] the number 295: "Out of the depths I cry to you", in your hymn book[153] the hymn number 456: «Из сердца глубины мой глас к Тебе», and in the hymn book of the Evangelical Lutheran Church of Russia[154] the hymn number 188: «Из сердца глубины мой глас». Martin Luther had written it according to Psalm 130 / Psalm 129: „Aus der Tiefe rufe ich, Herr, zu dir." – "Out of the depth I cry to thee, O Lord" – «Из глубины взываю к Тебе, Господи» (verse 1). I quote the second verse and the third verse of this hymn:

„Bei dir gilt nichts denn Gnad und Gunst,
die Sünde zu vergeben;
es ist doch unser Tun umsonst
auch in dem besten Leben.
Vor dir sich niemand rühmen kann,
des muss dich fürchten jedermann
und deiner Gnade leben.

"All things you send are full of grace;
you crown our lives with favor.
All our good works are done in vain
without our Lord and Savior.
We praise the God who gives us faith
and saves us from the grip of death;
our lives are in his keeping.

---

[149] Rainer Stahl: Die Evangelisch-Lutherische Kirche Ingriens auf dem Territorium Russlands, in: Lutherische Kirche in der Welt, Jahrbuch des Martin-Luther-Bundes, Folge 63, 2016, p. 193-219, especially p. 209-214, where I had also documented the 18 hymns by Martin Luther, from which only 10 hymns are documented in the hymn book of the Evangelical Lutheran Church in Russia (see below: note 16).
[150] Evangelisches Gesangbuch, Ausgabe für die Evangelisch-Lutherischen Kirchen in Bayern und Thüringen, für Thüringen: Wartburg Verlag, Weimar without year/1994.
[151] See: Laudamus. Hymnal for the Lutheran World Federation, Fifth edition, Budapest 1984.
[152] See: Lutheran Book of Worship, Minneapolis and Philadelphia 1978.
[153] Сборник Гимнов Евангелическо-лютеранской Церкви Ингрии на территории России, Санкт-Петербург 2013.
[154] Сборник песнопений Евангелическо-лютеранской Церкви, Санкт-Петербург 2009.

«Твоей лишь милостью мы все
спасенье обретаем,
И в самом праведном житье
Всё тщетно, что свершаем.
Хвалиться нечем пред Тобой.
Но Ты прощаешь – лишь одной[155]
Мы милости той чаем.

Darum auf Gott will hoffen ich,
auf mein Verdienst nicht bauen;
auf ihn mein Herz soll lassen sich
und seiner Güte trauen,
die mir zusagt sein wertes Wort;
das ist mein Trost und treuer Hort,
des will ich allzeit harren."

It is in God that we shall hope,
and not in our own merit.
We rest our fears in his good Word
and trust his Holy Spirit.
His promise keeps us strong and sure;
we trust the holy signature
inscribed upon our temples."

На Бога буду уповать,
Не на свои дела я,
Его святую благодать
Всем сердцем сознавая.
Мне в Слове благодать сия
Обещана, и верю я:
Она моя отрада.»

This early hymn explains a fundamental insight of Luther: We can understand our situation before God and our relation to God in two definitions:

+ We remain as persons with fundamental shortcomings in relation to God – the traditional theology speaks of "sin"!
+ Additional we remain as persons who have the most possible qualification, because God has declared us as justified persons!

Luther has said in this hymn: What we may do directed to God is without importance even in the best life: "All our good works are done in vain / without our Lord and Savior" – and is giving a solution: "with our Lord and Savior". Even the Russian translation recognizes the difficulties of our life which has to be overcome: «И в самом праведном житье / всё тщетно, что свершаем». But what we may do and should do in direction to our neighbor leads us into the necessary responsibility also in direction to God. On that way we exercise our trust in God's grace and support. This new insight makes me to a real Christian, makes me to a Lutheran.

---

[155] In the Russian hymn book (see note 154) these two lines are: «Кому хвалиться пред Тобой? / Но Ты простишь, и так одной».

May I look shortly to the melody. There I have to say: I do not understand much about music and melodies. I only can sing such hymns when I had learned the melodies. But I cannot explain the techniques. Because of that I only can inform you that Luther had composed a melody which expresses the deep affections of this hymn. In my German hymn Book we have two melodies – the first is from Martin Luther from 1524 and the second one from Wolfgang Dachstein, also from 1524. I only can try to demonstrate them to you. But you have a different melody, also explained as one from Martin Luther, 1524. I only can ask you to sing this melody of our hymn for me!

What is important and what I have deeply understood? The words and the melody are proclaiming the message together: The two verses, we have heard, show us that it's "only the grace by God" which opens us our new life: "All things you send are full of grace; you crown our lives with favor." – «Твоей лишь милостью мы все спасенье обретаем».[156]

I want to explain this from a more modern point of view: The British philosopher Bertrand Russell, who lived from 1872 to 1970, had given on May 6th, 1927, in London his paper "Why I Am Not a Christian". In this paper he had said: "We want to stand upon our own feet and look fair and square at the world – its good facts, its bad facts, its beauties, and its ugliness; see the world as it is and not be afraid of it. Conquer the world by intelligence […]."[157] I have the feeling that many persons think accordingly. They would say: "When I'm successful then I shall receive acknowledgement and even money." They take their lives into their own hands and forget to think of God. Luther would have answered, and Christians of our time would possibly answer: "These are important results within our earthly life. But even within it we cannot do anything without help – of other persons, of organizations, not without the support of the state, finally of God. And in view of our 'eternal' situation we are totally dependent of God's grace, of God's love! There we are in a responsibility we never could bear. There we need the help by God."

May I tell you a tiny story of my life in which I felt that I had received a help by God: Many years ago, in the deep years of the situation in the German Democratic Republic – in the year 1976 – I received even as a single person, as a non-married one, a small and simple apartment in Jena. In April 1976 I could move there. End

---

[156] Konrad Klek, op. cit. (see note 143), p. 19.
[157] Cf. https://de.wikipedia.org/wiki/Warum_ich_kein_Christ_bin; https://users.drew.edu/... /why-not.html – read on February 28th, 2020.

of August of that year I received a postcard by the police. They ordered me to a talk on Monday, September 6th, 1976. I was very uncertain and afraid: What the police will want from me? Who will meet me in that police office? Could it be possible, that even a person of the state security, of the „Staatssicherheit", will talk with me? But on Sunday, September 5th, the following Bible quote was read as the word of the week: „Das geknickte Rohr wird er nicht zerbrechen und den glimmenden Docht wird er nicht auslöschen" – "A bruised reed he will not break, and a dimly burning wick he will not quench" – «Трости надломленной не переломит, и льна курящегося не угасит» (Jesaja / Isaiah / Исаия 42:3). I still see myself sitting in the church and hearing this Biblical word. It was something like a revelation for me. Therefore by keeping this Bible word in my mind I went on the next day, on that Monday, to the police. And very quickly a policeman just asked whether my address is correct. Nothing else happened. After some minutes I was again in the street. No security, no „Staatssicherheit"! Was I happy that God's grace had been working with me!

II.2.

Now I want to turn to the "Marseille Hymn of the Reformation" – as the famous German and Jewish writer Heinrich Heine had called the hymn „Ein feste Burg ist unser Gott"[158] –, or the "Marseillaise of the farmers wars" – as Friedrich Engels the hymn had called[159] –. In our German hymn Book it has the number 362, in "Laudamus" the number 92b and in the "Lutheran Book of Worship" the numbers 228 and 229: "A mighty fortress is our God"[160], in your hymn book the number 222: «Господь нам крепость и оплот», translated by A. Grischin and A. Prilutzkij. This version of this important hymn we find also in the hymn book of the Lutheran Church of Russia under the number 217. But there is also another translation, that one by Anton Tichomirow: «Град крепкий – Бог наш, и оплот», hymn number 216.[161] But now we want to listen to the first verse and to the second verse of the translation by Grischin and Prilutzkij:

---

[158] Cf. Michael Fischer: „Ein feste Burg ist unser Gott". Ein Lied im Wandel der Zeiten, in: Peter Bubmann und Konrad Klek (Hg.), op. cit. (see note 143), p. 27-43, here: p. 40.
[159] See the short article by Maren Hellwig: »Ein feste Burg ist unser Gott«, in G+H 44 (the church newspaper of Central Germany), November 1st, 2020, p. 8.
[160] Between both texts in the "Lutheran Book of Worship" are some slight differences, which are not important for my interpretation (see below the discussion about verse 1b). One of the variants is identical with that one of "Laudamus".
[161] In the hymnal of the Evangelical Lutheran Church in Russia (see note 17) this hymn is also given in different languages. The English translation is slightly different from that one of the LWF form 1984, and also from that one of the "Lutheran Book of Worship".

„Ein feste Burg ist unser Gott
ein gute Wehr und Waffen.
Er hilft uns frei aus aller Not,
die uns jetzt hat betroffen.
Der alt böse Feind mit Ernst er's jetzt meint;

groß Macht und viel List sein grausam
Rüstung ist,
auf Erd ist nicht seinsgleichen.

"A mighty fortress is our God,
a sword and shield victorious;
He breaks the cruel oppressor's rod
and wins salvation glorious.
The old satanic foe has sworn
to work us woe!
With craft and dreadful might he arms
himself to fight.
On earth he has no equal.

«Господь нам крепость и оплот,
Он щит и меч надежный,
И нас спасает от невзгод
В сей день и час тревожный.
Враг древний зло таит, себя высоко мнит,
Своим лукавством он
Как в латы облечен,
Царит он над землею.

Mit unsrer Macht ist nichts getan,
wir sind gar bald verloren;
es streit' für uns der rechte Mann,
den Gott hat selbst erkoren.
Fragst du, wer der ist?
Er heißt Jesus Christ,
der Herr Zebaoth,
und ist kein andrer Gott,
das Feld muss er behalten."

No strength of ours can match his might!
We would be lost, rejected.
But now a champion comes to fight,
whom God himself elected.
You ask who this may be?
The Lord of hosts is he!
Jesus Christ, our Lord,
God's only Son adored.
He holds the field victorious."

Сражаться с войском темных сил
Никто из нас не может.
Но в битву ради нас вступил
Святой избранник Божий.
Кто есть воитель тот?
Иисус Христос, Господь,
Он Бог наш Саваоф,
И нет других богов.
Он нас ведет к победе.»

First we have to understand that Martin Luther had written a hymn which explains our faith and our trust on the basis of Psalm 46 / Psalm 45: „Gott ist unsre Zuversicht und Stärke" – "God is our refuge and strength" – «Бог нам прибежище и сила» (verse 1 or 2). For Martin Luther most important was that this psalm explains the trust in God and therefore the beginning of our feeling of thanks. And he had read this psalm as text about the Messiah and therefore had interpreted it as a text about Jesus Christ.[162] He had written this hymn for the Lenten time. He wanted to strengthen the behavior of sincerity and additionally of a serious way of life.[163] Only as the result of new developments our hymn has become a text and hymn of triumph and especially of German national success.[164]

Asking after the melody of „Ein feste Burg ist unser Gott", we have to realize that it underlines the trust, the feeling of thanks and of a self-critical reflection. That's original meaning I want to follow. It's really interesting that Martin Luther had not composed this melody alone, but he had asked his colleague for the area of church music, the famous cantor Johann Walter, to give council and be a cooperator. Without being able to say in detail what parts of the melody are from Luther and from Walter we can understand them as common creators of the melody or the melodies of this famous hymn.[165]

May I remember my father: He understood the not very clear word – "the old, bad enemy takes it seriously now" – as a word about the pope: there Luther had spoken mysteriously about the highest person of the Roman Church. I never had believed in this position. And now the Russian translation shows us what is meant here: «Враг древний зло таит» – literally: "the old, bad enemy is hiding himself". And under «враг» I have found in my small and old Langenscheidts dictionary from 1929 really also the term "devil". It was him about whom Luther had been spoken! And the English translations shows this too: "The old satanic foe has sworn to work us woe!" and: "The old evil foe, sworn to work us woe!".

Then I want to reflect especially about the second verse. For this I follow the translation into Russian we have heard, because this translation is very near to the German original. Martin Luther was speaking about Jesus Christ in a twofold way:

The first way to see on Jesus Christ tells us, that he is the right man, the person who God had chosen: „es streit' für uns der rechte Mann, / den Gott hat selbst erkoren" – "But now a champion comes to fight, / whom God himself elected" –

---

[162] Cf. Michael Fischer, op. cit., in: Peter Bubmann und Konrad Klek (Hg.), op. cit. (see note 143), p. 29.
[163] Cf. Michael Fischer, op. cit., in: Peter Bubmann und Konrad Klek (Hg.), op. cit. (see note 143), p. 30.
[164] Cf. Michael Fischer, op. cit., in: Peter Bubmann und Konrad Klek (Hg.), op. cit. (see note 143), p. 31-34.
[165] See Maren Hellwig, op.cit. (see note 159), there with the subtitle: „Komponierte Martin Luther oder Johann Walter die Melodie?" / „Did Martin Luther or Johann Walter compose the melody?"

«Но в битву ради нас вступил / Святой избранник Божий». And Anton Tichomirow had translated: «Но Божий Праведник один / За нас в борьбу вступает». In a similar way the English translation expresses this verse: "But now a champion comes to fight, whom God himself elected."

And in the second way to see on Jesus Christ tells us, that he is God himself. Here Luther had used a typical Hebrew term: יהוה צבאות – the "Lord of hosts" – «[…] Иисус Христос, Господь, / Он Бог наш Саваоф». And Anton Tichomirow translated: «[…] Иисус Христос, Господь, / Бог сил, Бог Саваоф». The English translation expresses: "The Lord of hosts is he! Christ Jesus, mighty Lord".

These together are very clear statements for the whole Christianity, for all churches, also for your Russian Orthodox Church: Jesus Christ was really a humankind, a human person, who lived on earth in a typical time – from 6 before Christ to 30 after Christ –, in a society we can search about – that one of the Jewish society within the Roman Empire –, because we can identify their details like we would work about an early predecessor of us.[166] And Jesus Christ is really the only God. We become Christians when we start to believe these both truths:
+ Jesus as a human being in a specific historical time and situation – Jesus Christ as a Jewish man in the Near East under the power of the Roman Empire.
+ And Jesus Christ as the only experience of God we have. Here I have to turn into the present time because about God we cannot speak only in the past time: As God is the real partner to all times, over all situations of our world.
But I have to add a commentary to both forms of truth: Jesus of Nazareth as a person of history needs not to be believed in, but only to be realized. But this Jesus of Nazareth as the Christ him has to be believed in!
May I repeat these sentences of Martin Luther:

| "[…] But now a champion comes to fight, whom God himself elected. You ask who this may be? The Lord of hosts is he! Christ Jesus, mighty Lord, […]" | «[…] Но в битву ради нас вступил Святой избранник Божий […] Иисус Христос, Господь, Он Бог наш Саваоф, И нет других богов. […]» |

But one sentence the translators have slightly changed: Luther had concluded the second verse with the comfort that God, that Christ will win. Or with the words of the English translation: "He holds the field victorious." In this way Anton

---

[166] See for example: Shimon Gibson: Die sieben letzten Tage Jesu. Die archäologischen Tatsachen, Munich 2010.

Tichomirow had translated: «За Ним победа будет!». But it's not said clearly what this victory will mean for us. And there the translators A. Grischin and A. Prilutzkij have turned just into this question: What the victory of Christ may mean for us? They have said that Christ, that God will offer us this victory: «Он нас ведет к победе». I think this is a wonderful comfort in the midst of our daily struggle!

Now I have to confess that the sequence from verse 3 to verse 4 for me for a long time was problematic. What Martin Luther had written?

„[…] Der Fürst dieser Welt,
wie saur er sich stellt,
tut er uns doch nicht;
das macht, er ist gericht':
ein Wörtlein kann ihn fällen.

"[…] Let this world's tyrant rage;
in battle we'll engage!
His might is doomed to fail;
God's judgement must prevail!
One little word subdues him.
[Or: "One little word can fell him."[167]]

«[…] Князь мира же сего
Не сможет ничего
Соделать нам в урон,
И суд над ним свершен –
Повержен был он Словом.
[Or: «Он проклят Божьим Словом!»[168]]

Das Wort sie sollen lassen stahn
und kein' Dank dazu haben;

er ist bei uns wohl auf dem Plan
mit seinem Geist und Gaben. […]."

God's Word forever shall abide,
no thanks to foes, who fear it;
[Or: "Nor any thanks have for it."[169]]
for God himself fights by our side
with weapons of the Spirit. […]."

И неизменен в Слове Бог –
Оно пребудет с нами […].»
[Or: «Господь воздаст нам во сто крат
За все потери наши.»[170]]

What is that „Wörtlein", this "little word", this «Словом» or this «Божьим Словом», how Anton Tichomirow had translated? And what's the relation of „das

---

[167] See the version of this hymn in the hymnal of the Evangelical Lutheran Church in Russia (see note 154).
[168] In the translation by Anton Tichomirow.
[169] Here again the version of this hymn in the hymnal of the Evangelical Lutheran Church in Russia (see note 154).
[170] This is the version by Anton Tichomirow.

Wort", "God's Word", «Слово Бог» to this „Wörtlein", to this "little word"? In several talks and discussions and exchanges I learned:

The "little word" might be for example the word "Amen" – «Аминь». A small word with which we express our trust in God – against all powers on earth which would like to have our trust. No, we trust in God – not in earthly powers! And the content of "the Word", or as it said in the English translation: of "God's Word", opens a certain relation: The sentence by Martin Luther is not related to "Thanks" but to an "Idea", to a "Thought", not to «Благодарность» but to «Мысль», to «Идея»! In German Luther had shortened the word „Gedanke" to „Dank" and wanted to say: We should not invest additional ideas, additional thoughts in the word of God but we should accept it![171] In that connection we realize that the translations – into English and into Russian – did not explain literally what Luther had said. But the interpreters produced thoughts by themselves – related to Luther's original. Only one hint I give: Only the two translations into English have used the term "thanks"!

What Martin Luther said with his sentence „und kein' Dank dazu haben" / "and they should not invest any additional thoughts" (may I try to translate the intention by Luther in this way), the first most important Church musician of the Lutheran Reformation, Johann Walter, had expressed in the first verse of his hymn „Allein auf Gottes Wort" from the year 1566, German hymn book number 195:

> „Auch menschlich Weisheit will ich nicht dem göttlich Wort vergleichen,
> was Gottes Wort klar spricht und richt', dem soll doch alles weichen."[172]

I only can try to translate this word into English:

> "Even human wisdom I won't compare with the Divine Word,
> what God's Word clearly proclaims and judges we should not flee."

During my paper on Reformations Day, October 31st, 2020, Martin Lieberknecht told, that his father liked to underline how precise the text of Luther has been: In

---

[171] I remember for example the note by Pastor Christoph Reinhold Morath after the worship service on October 25th, 2020, here in Erlangen. Anton Tichomirow underlined in his e-mail from November 5th, 2020, that the situation is really uncertain. He means, that it told that "they" in the beginning of verse 4 cannot have success.

[172] Here I have to add: „Das Evangelische Gesangbuch enthält wenigstens einen knappen Ausschnitt [...]" (cf. Martin Rößler, op. cit. (see note 139), p. 111. There are printed 4 verses on p. 112, of which the first one gives the idea of Martin Luther: „O Gott, lass mich kein falsche Lehr / von deiner Wahrheit trennen, / hilf mir um deines Namens Ehr / die Wahrheit zu bekennen".

verse 3 Martin Luther had expressed the human stability against the evil, against The Evil with the verb „sollen": „es soll uns doch gelingen". And in verse 4 he had expressed the final conviction of our hope of faith: „das Reich muss uns doch bleiben". Both ways tell – in diversity of the themes – that the salvation is a gift to us: Where Luther was speaking about our ability he said „sollen" – the result will not be only within our hands. Where Luther was speaking about a real gift, for what we cannot do anything, he said „muss" – besides of all our misdeeds there is the hope of the Kingdom of God. It's interesting how the different translators have formulated these short sentences:

The German original:

Verse 3: „[…] es <u>soll</u> uns doch gelingen.
Verse 4: „[…] das Reich <u>muss</u> uns doch bleiben."

The English translation in the "Laudamus":
Vers 3: "[…] they cannot overpow'r us."
Vers 4: "The Kingdom'<u>s</u> ours forever!" – With "to be".

The English translation which is in the Russian hymn book:
Vers 3: "They <u>shall</u> not overpower us."
Vers 4: "[…] the Kingdom ours remaineth". – A simple statement of being.

The Russian translation by Anton Tichomirow:
Vers 3: «За прочною стеною» – "Behind a firm wall".
Vers 4: «Своё дарует царство!» – "He will give his Kingdom!"

The Russian translation by A. Grischin and A. Priluzkij:
Vers 3: «Господь нас не оставит» – "The Lord will not leave us".
Vers 4: «Наследники мы Царства» – "Inheritors of the Kingdom are we".

I think it's very interesting to see in connection with one example how this moving and powerful text of Martin Luther was understood. There we realize its liveliness – the liveliness of these texts![173]

---

[173] Only as a footnote I'm referring to a question which was said on October 31st, 2020: We understand today the formulation of verse 4 as problematic (that the wife was mentioned as the last person), but it seems to be a quote from the Ban bull „Decet Romanum Pontificem" of January 3rd, 1521: „Nehmen sie den Leib, Gut, Ehr, Kind und Weib". Martin Luther had expressed in his hymn what the opponents had threatened. The English translations tell these formulations: "Were they to take our house,/ goods, honor, child or spouse" ("Laudamus"); "And take they our life, / Goods, fame, child and wife" (Russian Hymn Book). The Russian translations says this more freely and does not touch the problematic details: «От века нас избрав / И к святости призвав» [„For Eternity our choice / and called to holiness"] (Anton Tichomirow); «Пускай разрушит враг / Наш кров и наш очаг» [„Does destroy the devil the beginning / our blood and our stove"] (A. Grischin und A. Priluzkij).

May I conclude this part with an additional observation, we can make in the Hungarian people: The normal formulation for "Hello" – «Добрый День» is: „Jó napot kivánok". But conscious Christians greet each other with a typical sentence, a sentence according to the confession they belong to. On June 18th, 2011, I could represent the Martin-Luther-Bund in Györ, former: Raab, where Bishop János Ittzés ended his service as bishop. At the end of the worship service, I gave a word of greetings and had prepared these different ways of greetings concerning the confessional traditions. I started with the greeting of our Roman-Catholic friends, because a Roman-Catholic bishop was present: „Discértessék a Jézus Krisztus!" – "Praised be Jesus Christ!". Immediately the also present Reformed Bishop, sitting in front of me in the first row, looked annoyed. But after all had answered „Mindörökké, Ámen!" – "In Eternity, Amen!". I greeted also in the Reformed way: „Áldás Békesség!" – "Blessing and Peace!". Again, immediately the Reformed bishop looked in a special way, but now very happy. The congregation answered a sentence, I did not understand. And finally I greeted in our Lutheran way: „Erős vár a mi Istenünk!" – «Господь нам крепость и оплот!» This greeting I have had the privilege to learn in the year 2001 after a worship service in Romania with Bishop Árpád Mózes in the parish Hălmeag (in the Romanian language) / Halmágy (in the Hungarian language) / Halmagen (in the German language). In Siebenbürgen, the northern part of Romania, more or less each place has his name in three languages – Romanian, Hungarian and German. After the worship service by saying "Hello!" at the churches door each parishioner – may be nearly hundred persons! – said to me: „Erős vár a mi Istenünk!", and I answered with: „Erős vár a mi Istenünk!" – «Господь нам крепость и оплот!» Since then I know this important Hungarian word: „Erős vár a mi Istenünk!" – «Господь нам крепость и оплот!» Isn't this a wonderful tradition?!

II.3.

Now we want to go into the year 1542, the fifth year before Martin Luther's death. The political situation of Europe was difficult – because news did go around that the Turks would prepare a new aggression against Europe, and the king of France and even the Pope seemed to reflect about an alliance with the Turks against the Roman Empire, against Germany! Please imagine such a possibility! In this situation Martin Luther wrote his hymn which now in the German hymn Book has the number 193, in "Laudamus" the number 89, in the "Lutheran Book of Worship" the number 230, and in your hymn book the number 281. Additional I underline that in the hymn book of the Lutheran Church of Russia under number 236 the similar text is documented like in your hymn book!

But in all three variants the real original version of its first verse is not documented. That's why I'm starting with this original text:

„Erhalt uns, Herr, bei deinem Wort und steur des Papstes und Türken Mord."[174]	"Lord, keep us steadfast in your Word; and limit the murder of the Pope and the Turks."[175]

May I try to give this in Russian language:

«Сохрани нас, Господи, в Слове Твоём.
И останови убийства, творимые Папой и Турками.»[176]

Here Martin Luther had mentioned the Muslims and the Roman Catholics in one line. Today we never can follow such a formulation. We have to look at our Turkish and Muslim neighbors and at our Christian sisters and brethren within the Roman Catholic Church in a behavior of dialogue and of cooperation. I'm really thankful that we now use in this hymn a more general wording. But what we still need is to identify ourselves with our Christian conviction, to know about it as much as possible, to bring it into an open and tolerant discussion together with others. But before we may listen to the present version of the first verse of our hymn I underline that your Russian tradition starts in line one slightly different: "Give us the blessed Word" – I understand. But I would say in your language: «Сохранай, Господь, Слово Твоего благодать». After these observations and ideas we now want to listen to the present version of this first verse of our hymn:

„Erhalt uns, Herr, bei deinem Wort und steure deiner Feinde Mord, die Jesus Christus, deinen Sohn, wollen stürzen von deinem Thron."	"Lord, keep us steadfast in your Word; curb those who by deceit or sword would wrest the kingdom from your Son and bring to nought all he has done."

«Даруй нам Слова благодать;
срази Ты, Отче, вражью рать,
когда она дерзнет на власть
престола Твоего напасть.»

---

[174] Cf. again Martin Rößler, op. cit. (see note 139), p. 73.
[175] This English version I tried to formulate.
[176] This translation I could realize by help of Anton Tichomirow, St. Petersburg, cf. his e-mail from July 27th, 2020.

Here Martin Luther is teaching us that the word of God is the most important gift of the Reformation. He was convinced that this word always is active and is bringing results. Even – imagine this – in political dangerous situations, like that one Luther just was reflecting on. There he had written such hymn and hoped that all who will sing it will find refuge within fear and uncertainty. And – as I had read in the article by Martin Rößler – he had suggested that pupils, youngsters should sing this hymn to bring and to win courage![177]

I would like to underline one special detail in the German original, from which I do not know exactly whether your Russian version from the Lutheran Hymn Book from 1915 has expressed it. Martin Luther in the year 1542 wrote:

„[…] die Jesus Christus, <u>deinen</u> Sohn,

wollen stürzen von <u>deinem</u> Thron."

"[…] who wrest the kingdom from <u>your</u> Son

and bring to nought all he has done."

Important would be: "<u>your</u> son" and "will be thrown from <u>your</u> throne". The English translation is relatively free and says that the enemies of Christ would change all his deeds into nothing. The Russian translation follows some typical ways:

«[…] когда она дерзнет на власть
престола Твоего напасть.»

There you also have "<u>your</u> throne" – «престола Твоего» –, but you do not express precisely Christ as the Son of the Father who is addressed! But the following is really said: The Lord we do believe does exist on the throne of God, is our God, will lead us in our lives in a good and wonderful way. Please allow me to invite you to such a belief, to such a trust, to such a deep conviction for your lives!

III.

You have already realized that I had started with hymns by Martin Luther, which are translated into the Russian language and published in the hymn book of your Ingrian Church. There is also one very important hymn: „Wir glauben all an einen Gott" – "We all believe in one true God" – «Мы в Бога веруем Отца», which has in my German Hymn book the number 183, in your hymn book the number 452, but what is not included into the hymn book of the Evangelical Lutheran Church in Russia, either not included into "Laudamus". But we find it as number

---

[177] Cf. Martin Rößler, op. cit. (see note 139), p. 73.

374 in the "Lutheran Book of Worship". Martin Luther had published this hymn in 1524 but did not write a melody for it. This hymn expresses the convictions in three verses. In the beginning we look at the first verse:

„Wir glauben all an einen Gott,	"We all believe in one true God,
Schöpfer Himmels und der Erden,	Who created earth and heaven,
der sich zum Vater geben hat,	The Father, who to us in love
dass wir seine Kinder werden. […]"	Has the right of children given. […]"

«Мы в Бога веруем Отца
Пусть Его святитя имя!
Он истинный великий Бог,
нас назвал детьми Своими […].»

We see that the English translation is very near to the German original and focuses on the fact that the humankind can understand themselves as being children of God. Then I underline that the second line is given in your Russian translation in a different way: Luther was speaking about God, the creator of heaven and earth. Your Lutheran translation does express in this verse the importance of the holy name of God.

To this verse we can say: By speaking about God we are not interested in "scientific neutral statements" – as I may say –, but we are interested in our relation to this God. To believe in God has the aim to understand ourselves, to understand ourselves from the basis of our relation to God who gives us inner security and trust. You may see that I understand myself within the present theology after the so called "anthropological turn": Our theological question of God will happen on the field of anthropology, and our anthropology has to have – if it wants to be really powerful, really meaningful – a theological Centre![178] Then we realize: How Luther had formulated this verse we only can understand on the basis of this direct relation of sentences about God and of sentences about humankind – God "the Father […] has the right of children given" – the «истинный великий Бог» has «нас назвал детьми Своими»!

Verse two: „Wir glauben auch an Jesus Christ,   "We all believe in Jesus Christ,
seinen Sohn und unsern Herren,   His own Son, our Lord, possessing
der ewig bei dem Vater ist,   An equal Godhead, throne, and might,
gleicher Gott von Macht und Ehren […]."   Source of ev'ry grace and blessing […]."

---

[178] Cf. Markus Knapp: Öffentliche Vernunft – religiöse Vernunft, p. 203-224, especially p. 216, in: Knut Wenzel, Thomas M. Schmidt (Ed.): Moderne Religion? Theologische und religionsphilosophische Reaktionen auf Jürgen Habermas, Freiburg 2009.

> «Во Иисуса веруем Христа.
> Божий Сын Единородный
> за грех наш жертвою предстал,
> от греха нам дал свободу. […]»

The English version is very near to the German original, but it turns the importance to that one what we receive from God: "grace and blessing". In your Russian translation one detail is interesting: Martin Luther had given terms about the divine essence of Jesus Christ: He is eternal together with the divine Father, he is the similar God of power and glory. Your tradition of translation had spoken about the consequences for us: That Christ was active against our sin, that he had given us freedom from our sin! This means: Christ frees us from our behavior, which urges us to forget God! I think: Who is able to say this and to sing this is showing with new words that these Jesus Christ really is similar to God!

Verse three: „Wir glauben an den Heilgen Geist,	"We all confess the Holy Ghost
Gott mit Vater und dem Sohne,	who, in highest heaven dwelling
der aller Schwachen Tröster heißt	with God the Father and the Son,
und mit Gaben zieret schöne […]."	comforts us beyond all telling […]."

> «И во Святого Духа веруем:
> нас хранит от искушений
> и нам среди земных сует
> Он дарует утешенье. […]»

Concerning the translation into English I want to underline one detail: We do not believe in the Holy Ghost but we confess him! And all three versions – in German, in English and in Russian – turn to the consequences for us, the Christians: This Spirit is keeping us in dangers and sorrows. And at the end again the Spirit is explained as helper that we may receive the salvation of our unique faith. In the same way Martin Luther also was reflecting about the meaning of the Holy Spirit: that he – may I also say: "she"? – clearly is God together with the Father and the Son, and that he, that "she" is comforting us!

There we see that the main aim of this hymn is to find words for the typical Christian faith in the Triune God. Many persons outside of Christianity do not understand this: "What is that – the Triune God?" They think that we Christians would believe in three Gods. But this is not correct. We believe really in the one and only God. But we are convinced that this one and only God is acting in three persons, in three possibilities to experience him – as I may use this very human term: to experience him. These three possibilities to experience him, these three persons are: The first is the Spirit, the second is the Father and the third is the Son. May I try to explain this theology of mystery in this new sequence. And when I try to explain this very shortly I want to quote a colleague, Pastor Sebastian Führer in Leipzig, who had written a meditation to Romans 6:12-18 on March 6th, 2020, beginning with verse 18: „Denn indem ihr nun frei geworden seid von der Sünde, seid ihr Knechte geworden der Gerechtigkeit" – "And, having been set free from sin, have become slaves of righteousness" – «Освободившись же от греха, вы стали рабами праведности». In his meditation he had formulated three short sentences, which may be of help for us in that difficult field:[179]

The Spirit confronts us with the truth by insights, by what we are reading in the Bible, by theological teachings, by poems – even by hymns –, by art like paintings and so on. Sebastian Führer wrote: „Mit dem Heiligen Geist verbunden zu bleiben, heißt, mich von ihm leiten zu lassen." – "Being connected with the Holy Spirit means being guided by him."

The Father assures us that we are created, that each of us has an importance, that God wanted me! Luke who had written the Acts had reported an interesting statement by St. Paul in Athens: „Dass sie Gott suchen sollen […] und fürwahr, er ist nicht ferne von einem jeden von uns. Denn in ihm leben, weben und sind wir […]" – "That they should seek God […] Yet he is not far from each one of us, for 'In him we live and move and have our being' […]" – «Дабы они искали Бога […] и не далеко от каждого из нас: Ибо мы Им живем и движемся и существуем […]» (Acts / Деяния 17:27-28). Here Sebastian Führer expressed: „An Jahwe, an Gott gebunden zu bleiben, heißt, seine Gebote zu erfüllen." – "Being bound to Jahwe, to God means to fulfill his commandments." That's correct, and an additional importance will become for us, when we understand us really in relation to God: Without him I would not be, would not be one single day of my life!

The Son opens us a twofold relation to God. It's cleary expressed by Martin Luther within the verse on Jesus from Nazareth, on Jesus Christ, on the Son: First we had heard, that he is eternal with the divine Father, the similar God of power and glory. And now Martin Luther underlined within his second verse, which I may quote again:

---

[179] "Feste-Burg-Kalender" for the year 2020, edited by Wolfgang Schmidt: Meditation for March 6th, 2020.

„[…] ist ein wahrer Mensch geboren durch den Heiligen Geist im Glauben […]."

"[…] Born of Mary, virgin mother, By the power of the Spirit […]."

«[…] Человеком стал Он, как и мы, дал нам радость жизни новой […].»

This dimension is very important: When we speak about Jesus of Nazareth, about Jesus Christ, we always have to have these two dimensions in mind: He was really a human being. Here the English translation underlines the miraculous aspect of this human birth. And he was and is for eternity really God. These dimensions we cannot explain logically. But to become a Christian and to continue being a Christian we have to hold together these two dimensions! And about them Sebastian Führer wrote: „An Jesus gebunden zu bleiben, heißt, ihn zurückzulieben." – "Being bound to Jesus means to react to his love with my love." And what else might be important than a relation of love! We are already loved, and now we react on the way of our love.

Even for us Christians: no picture for God! Exodus 32:1-6.15-20[180]

"The grace of our Lord Jesus Christ,
the love of God
and the fellowship of the Holy Spirit be with you all. Amen."

Dear Sisters and Brothers!

Maybe ten years ago I discovered in one of the antiquarian bookshops at the Leipzig book fare a book which impressed me immediately: from the year 1924, from Uriel Birnbaum: „Moses".[181] The author had reported the unity of the Biblical stories about Moses in an impressive way:

„Er führte das Volk der Feuersäule nach zu dem Berge der Berufung, er stieg empor zu dem flammenden Gipfel, blieb vierzig Tage dort oben, dem Volke durch feuriges Gewölk verborgen, und sprach mit Gott. Er mit Menschenhänden nahm aus Gottes eigenen Händen die Tafeln des Bundes und zerschlug im Zorne die Handschrift des Herrn. Er […] zermalmte das goldene Kalb und verbrannte den Goldstaub und zwang höhnisch seinen eigenen abtrünnigen Bruder – den Hohepriester – den Schwächling, die Asche zu trinken." – "He guided the people behind the column of fire to the mountain of Calling. He climbed to the burning peak and stayed there for 40 days, hidden to the people by the burning clouds. And he was talking with God. He with his human hands received from Gods own hands the tablets of the Covenant and destroyed in anger the handwriting of the Lord. He […] crushed the Golden Calf and burned the golden dust and ordered his own sinful brother – the High Priest – to drink the ash."[182] At that day by buying this book it was the sequence of the illustrations which impressed me.

Each picture has below a double line frame with the main formulations of the biblical scene.
On the picture of the calf: אלה אלהיך ישראל אשר העלוך מארץ מצרים – «'elläh 'älohäjcha jisra'el 'aschär häᶜälucha me'äräz mizrajim» – "These are your gods,

---
[180] This sermon was given on Ash Wednesday, March 2nd, 2022, in the Roman-Catholic Church „St. Heinrich" in Erlangen. And a longer version was given to the homepage of „Göttinger Predigten im Internet".
[181] Ein biblischer Zyklus in fünfzig Bildern mit einem einleitenden Essay, Thyrsos-Verlag, Wien und Berlin 1924.
[182] Uriel Birnbaum, op. cit. (note 181), p. 19-20 (The translation into English was made by myself.).

O Israel, who brought you up out of the land of Egypt!" (verse 4). And then the artist quoted additionally (verse 6): "And they rose up early on the morrow, and offered burnt offerings and brought peace offerings; at the people sat down to eat and drink, and rose up to play."

It's really impressive that the artist painted the picture of the bull very big, but the persons who adored him really tiny[183], that I have to ask the question: How could have Aaron formed such statue with the ear-rings of these tiny people?

And on the following page, directly right of that one we have just seen, the artist had painted Moses how he realized this bull-statue and the festivity of the people:

Under this picture he had quoted: וירא את העגל ומחלת – «wajjar' 'äth ha ͨegäl umcholoth» – "He saw the calf and the dancing" (verse 19). And then the last part of this verse: "and Moses' anger burned hot, and he threw the tables out of his hands and broke them at the foot of the mountain."

---

[183] Op. cit. (note 181), p. 56.

Now the statue of the calf – seen from behind – is smaller and the dancing people very tiny, but Moses really tall and full of emotions.[184]

I would like to read an interesting interpretation by Uriel Brinbaum: „Und wie jung gar sind Christentum und Islam – und dabei sind doch letzten Endes beide Weltreligionen selbst nur große Erweiterungen des ursprünglichen Stromes […]. Er wird noch […] in vielen Tälern sich stauen und viele Schluchten durchbrausen […]. Aber nie mehr kann er versiegen, nie mehr eingedämmt werden […] bis die Erkenntnis des wahren Gottes, wie sie Mose als erstem zur Gänze zu Teil wurde, sich ausgebreitet haben wird über alle Menschen […]." – "And how young are Christianity and Islam – but finally both world religions are only a way to broad the original stream […]. It will […] jam up in many valleys and rush through many canyons […]. But never it can dry up, never being contained […] until the recognition of the true God, whom Moses as first man had recognized, will spread over the whole humankind […]."[185]

What was said here in Exodus is shaped by the recognition of the oneness and the singularity of God. We see this especially through the way how about the cult-decision of Aaron was told: "These are your gods, O Israel who brought you up out of the land of Egypt!" (verse 4). Really in plural: אלה – «'elläh» – "these", not "he", not "this". Or even before: "Up, make us gods, who shall go before us […]" (verse 1). About all of such challenges this Bible word want to warn us.

In this connection I was impressed by the deep confidence of the faith of Uriel Birnbaum in the Twenties of the last century: „[…] bis die Erkenntnis des wahren Gottes […] sich ausgebreitet haben wird über alle Menschen […]." / "[…] until the recognition of the true God, whom Moses as first man had recognized, will spread over the whole humankind […]."[186] This matters – especially today! For that we are called: The recognition of the unity of God! – Only: He! Instead of him: Nothing!

We have understood the pictures by Uriel Birnbaum. Therefore, I would like to show another experience of a picture: In Nuremberg a small church was renovated and converted to the Cathedral of the Metropolis of the Romanian Orthodox

---

[184] Op. cit. (note 181), p. 57.
[185] Op. cit. (note 181), p. 15 (The translation into English was made by myself.).
[186] Only here I want to underline, that Uriel Birnbaum, born on November 13th, 1894, in Vienna, could escape with difficulties from the murdering machine – because he could hide himself from 1943 to 1945. He died in December 1956 in Amersfoort, the Netherlands. Cf.: https://de.wikipedia.org/wiki/Uriel_Birnbaum (read on January 29th, 2022).

Church for Germany and Central Europe. Until 2006 Grigore Popescu and Maria Popescu painted it. Some years ago, I could visit this church for a sanctification of a deacon. And all these paintings impressed me very much.

Especially at the western wall a life tree with pictures of confessors of Christ – many martyrs of the orthodox tradition, but also pictures of Reverend Paul Schneider (murdered in 1939) and of Reverend Dietrich Bonhoeffer (murdered in 1945)! But even of Edith Stein (murdered in 1942), of the farmer Franz Jägerstätter (murdered in 1943) and of Father Maximilian Kolbe (murdered in 1941)! Then the colleague, who was sanctified as deacon in that worship service – Father Jonuţ Paun, now priest in Bamberg – has dedicated to me a wonderful book about all paintings of this church.[187]

What I realized by studying this book? What is very important in that church? There do not exist any pictures of God the Father! The only picture of God that is the picture of Jesus Christ – and this exists several times! At the barrel vault between the dome and the western wall of the Apsis there exists an impressive painting of Pentecost, of the giving of the Holy Spirit to the disciples:[188]

There the Artists have painted the Trinity through three different kinds of Red in one circle, out of this the power lines of the Spirit go to the heads of the disciples! Therefore, I'm inviting you: Please follow the faith in the undrawing God! We are especially near to God, when we keep him mysterious – and trust in his decisions and his way with us! All pictures are kinds of help to practice this trust.

---

[187] Rumänische Orthodoxe Kathedrale Nürnberg. Freskenmalerei und Geschichte, ed. by Grigore and Maria Popescu, Cluj-Napoca – Klausenburg 2009.
[188] Grigore and Maria Popescu, op. cit. (see note 187) p. 42 and 43.

And this trust we have to fulfill especially when we have nothing in our hands. When the fear for our health and our life dominates us. When we have to go on our last earthly way. When sisters and doctors take care of us in a good way, but the result will be uncertain. Then to grasp the truth that the unseen God will not leave us – that's important. Like one time, as I had to go to a new chemical treatment into the hospital, it was said to me: "We at the station are lucky, that you are coming!" And one male nurse said to me: "Oh, you have your »Daily Watchwords«, your »Moravian Daily Texts« with you!" Such kinds of faith God will answer in a positive way!
Amen.

"And the peace of God which passes all understanding,
will keep your hearts and your minds in Christ Jesus."

"You shall live!"
Ezekiel 37:1-14[189]

"The grace of our Lord Jesus Christ,
the love of God
and the fellowship of the Holy Spirit be with you all. Amen."

Dear Sisters and Brothers!

This story in Ezekiel 37 – the vision of the valley, full of bones – is very strange for us. But it gave remembrance to an experience, I had a long time ago: Our small group of the so called "Learning tour" – four participants from the GDR and two participants from Switzerland – was on September 8th, 1989, on tour along the Euphrates to Mari in Eastern Syria. On that tour we also made a short visiting stop in the ruins of the town Dura Europos. In the 2nd century after Christ the Roman Empire could conquer this town – you should imagine this! – and made it to a part of the Syrian Limes. But already in the midst of the 3rd century after Christ the army of the Persian Empire reconquered it. And since that time it's a ruin. It was possible to find interesting ruins from the Roman time, which had been kept under rubble, with what the town wall was secured: At the southwestern town wall two houses in nearly similar distance to the main gate of the town – restructured as meeting places of two Religious Communities. When you have come through the town gate and went to left, to northwest, you would had found a living complex in which a Synagogue was built. And when you have gone to right, to southeast, nearly the same distance from the town gate, you would had found a living complex in which a Christian House Church was built.[190]

This situation has a deep meaning for me: At the edge of the town, directly near the town wall, at the same street – which shows their deep relationship –: Synagogue and Church. But in the middle of the town, in the middle of the society: the temple for Artemis and the temples for Gods which had come from Palmyra: the temple for Atargatis and the temple for Gods which belonged to the group of the "Lord of Heaven". The two Religious Houses became interesting because frescoes have been found in them: Biblical scenes in the Church and in the Synagogue a total wall painting:

---

[189] This sermon was written for the Holy Saturday, April 4th, 2022, and sent to the homepage of „Göttinger Predigten im Internet".
[190] Please see: Johannes Odenthal: Syrien. Hochkulturen zwischen Mittelmeer und Arabischer Wüste – 5000 Jahre Geschichte im Spannungsfeld von Orient und Okzident, Köln ⁴1988, p. 288-293.

For example, the childhood of Moses, the way of the Israelites through the sea, the enthronement of David, the temple of Jerusalem, a picture of Isaiah <u>and also</u>: Ezekiel in the valley of bones! This fresco combines some scenes and shows Ezekiel on our detail three time. For example: God puts Ezekiel into the valley. And the fact that the heads and arms and legs have skin, show that the mystery is under process. The hands which come from above into the picture we have to understand as the hands of God.[191]

On September 21st, 1989 we have been in the museum in Damascus and could see the reconstruction of the gathering room of the Synagogue – all painting wonderfully restored. At its original place this wonderful art was maybe only for ten years. And within it this scene of this death field, from which the bones will be revitalized!

In front of this painting, we understand the fundamental importance of this scene: Each Jewish community lives in the consciousness, that God will give future. Through many threats and dangers, and out of them: On October 9th, 2019, I was travelling to an Old Testament meeting together with colleagues in Halle. I came some hours later, because the train from Erlangen had to go a longer way. And in the meeting the colleague from Halle had to inform us, that the streets are blocked, trains could not go elsewhere, all was blocked: Because an assassin had tried to enter the Synagogue and attack the parish of the festivity of Jom Kippur.[192] But the door of the Synagogue stopped the assassin.[193]

---

[191] See a paper I had found into the Internet: Petra Sevrugian: Kurt Weizmann und Herbert L. Kessler, The Frescoes of the Dura Synagogue and Christian Art, p. 702. The picture I have found in: https://www.google.com/search?q=Synagoge+Dura+Europos+Bild+Ezechiel+37... (seen on February 6th, 2022).
[192] To the festivity of יום כפור or יום כפורים see only Leviticus 16.
[193] See: https://de.wikipedia.org/wiki/Anschlag_in_Halle_(Saale)_2019 (read on February 7th, 2022).

In the evening I could participate in a peace prayer in the Market-Church and very early on the next morning I could travel back to Erlangen. But the assassin had murdered two bystanders and wounded two others. This meant: Being kept and being destroyed have taken place on the same day. I have the feeling, that our scene in the book of Ezekiel often confronts us with this tension!

But now: How I can preach this scene as a Christian? What message this scene may have for our worldwide community of Christian believers? Because the most important point of this scene – the resurrection of the People of God, of the People Israel (!) – does not refer to us as Christians, as the community of the many-confessional, the international Church. That's the content for our Jewish friends!

I see two ways:
+ First the question, whether and how authors of our New Testament have taken it up. Fundamentally we have to underline: The Hebrew Bible is only for us as Christians the "Old Testament". Because it needs our decision to want to be Christians!
+ And then the question, to which moment in the church year this scene should ordered!
+ The first question: I always check in my new edition of the Greek New Testament, where we can see innuendos or literal quotations.[194]
In his report about the crucifixion of Jesus Christ the Evangelist Matthew gives important hints. Under them: That in the very moment, in which Jesus died, many graves were opened and the dead people stood up (Matthew 27:52). What in the scene of Ezekiel 37:12-13 was expected, will start as "accompanying music" to the dying of Jesus. There new life already starts!

And: In nearly the same time of Matthew the Seer John had written his great work of the "Revelation". There he reported the story about the two witnesses who shall prophesy. They will be murdered by "the beast that ascends from the bottomless pit". But finally, "breath of life from God" will enter into them (Revelation 11:7.11). There John had used deliberately the words of Ezekiel 37:5 and 37:10: "And the breath came into them, and they lived"!

Both pictures of hope show for our existence as Christians: It was done very much in the beginning, during the sacrifice of Jesus Christ. And it was done very much

---

[194] See: Nestle – Aland: Novum Testamentum Graece, founded by Eberhard and Erwin Nestle, ed. by Barbara and Kurt Aland, Johannes Karavidopoulos, Carlo M. Martini and Bruce M. Metzger, 28. Revised Edition, Stuttgart 2012.

in the end, with a totally new fulfilling: "The kingdom of the world has become the kingdom of our Lord and of his Christ, and he shall reign for ever and ever" (Revelation 11:15b).

+ The second question: But the women and men, who are in our time responsible for the Bible texts for each Sunday have ordered our scene to the Holy Saturday, not to the story of the dying of Jesus, and not to the beginning of a new life under the power of the resurrected – then not "only" for the believing but as a reality, which will be experienced by all!

What can I preach for the "in between"? I only can understand the scene in Ezekiel as a huge horizon over our "small" changes: When we have been sick, but it was possible to help us and we could return to our daily life, we will remain in this life, which will go into the death. But even this return into our daily life we can understand as a wonderful experience of being kept by God, as a "New Creation" by God! Therefore, some celebrate the day of recovery from hard sickness as a "new birthday"! On that way they have understood that God has sent "the breath into them, and they lived, and stood upon their feet" (Ezekiel 37:10).
Amen.

"And the peace of God which passes all understanding,
will keep your hearts and your minds in Christ Jesus."

Jonah 2, Meditation for the Workshop of Sermons of the Luther-Convent in the Evangelical Church in the Rhineland[195]

1. Jonah 1:17 – 2:10 / 2:1-11[196]

"[17]And the Lord appointed a great fish to swallow up Jonah; and Jonah was in the belly of the fish three days and three nights. [1]Then Jonah prayed to the Lord his God from the belly of the fish, [2]saying,
»I called to the Lord, out of my distress, and he answered me; out of the belly of Sheol I cried, and thou didst hear my voice.
[3]For thou didst cast me into the deep, into the heart of the seas, and the flood was round about me; all thy waves and thy billows passed over me.
[4]Then I said, 'I am cast out from thy presence; how shall I again look upon thy holy temple?'
[5]The waters closed in over me, the deep was round about me; weeds were wrapped about my head
[6]at the roots of the mountains.
I went down to the land whose bars closed upon me for ever; yet thou didst bring up my life from the Pit, o Lord my God.
[7]When my soul fainted within me, I remembered the Lord; and my prayer came to thee, into thy holy temple.
[8]Those who pay regard to vain idols forsake their true loyalty.
[9]But I with the voice of thanksgiving will sacrifice to thee; what I have vowed I will pay. Deliverance belongs to the Lord!«
[10]And the Lord spoke to the fish, and it vomited out Jonah upon the dry land."

1. Aspects of an exegetical view:

In Jesus Sirach 49,10 we found the following statement: "Also the twelve prophets, may their bones flourish again […]. He comforted the people of Jacob, and delivered them by confident hope". Jesus Sirach had in the time in which he was working – in the 2. century before Christ, around 175 before Christ, the collection of the Twelve Prophets already in front of himself. And this means: Even the novel about the prophet of Jonah, what means "dove", a word with which called him "stupid". I'm quoting: "Ephraim is like a dove, silly and without sense […]" (Hosea 7:11). This novel should be written in the end of the 2. century before

---

[195] This paper was given for the Easter Monday, April 18th, 2022.
[196] Contrary to the Masoretic Text and to the Septuagint the Revised Standard Version has counted verse 1 of chapter 2 as verse 17 of chapter 1.

Christ or in the beginning of the 3. century before Christ (seen from us back into the past). The book describes sketches about the remembrance of the unity and the peace order of the Persian Empire, but seems to be written after the destruction of that empire and during the time of insecurity and oppression in the following Greek kingdoms and their conflicts around 300 before Christ. Against this background we can understand, that the authors referred to the first international empire, the Assyrian Empire: The citizens of Nineveh and the king of the world power react to the very small sermon of Jonah (Jonah 3:4b) with immediate and radical repentance. This situation leads to an international expression of the faith: God is the Redeemer for all people (Jonah 3:10). But Jonah was painted as one, who still has to learn a fundamental lesson, a task, which he will not fulfill in this novel (see: Jonah 4:1-11).

In Jonah 2:1-10 a psalm is given, prayed in the body of a fish (so the Masoretic Bible) or in the body of a sea monster (so the Septuagint). Only a few of the scholars understand it as secondary. It seems that this psalm was part of the novel from the very beginning. But – what will become important for this sermon – it broadens the meaning far over the person of Jonah and the situation in a fish or in a sea monster until existential dangers for each one of us: Because these challenges are described as "the belly of Sheol" (verse 2), as "the heart of the seas" (verse 3), that the "weeds were wrapped about my head at the roots of the mountains" (verses 5-6). What gives us possibilities to explain our fear during the war in the Ukraine.

2. Possible ways of meditation

2.1. All ways to understand this strange existence in the body of a fish or of a sea monster as a scientific possible are for me wrong ways. In the Internet you can find a story of a whale catcher who was swallowed by a whale but survived – his colleagues murdered the whale and had cut out this man.[197] But this wife – you can find this information also in the Internet – had always argued against this story: Her husband – James Bartley – died in 1909 and was never swallowed by a whale.[198] This confirms in a wonderful way the experience of the diver Rainer Schimpf, who was caught by a whale on March 11th, 2019, but quickly spited out: "It became suddenly dark, I felt pressure on my hip, and I knew: A whale has

---

[197] Cf.: ttps://jonateam.de/aus-aller-welt/56-walfaenger-ueberlebt-24-stunden-im-bauch-eines-wals, read on March 24th, 2019.
[198] Cf.: https://en.wikipedia.org/wiki/James_Bartley, also read on March 24th, 2019.

grabbed me!" "But Rainer Schimpf was happy: The whale was a baleen whale, and he was not his food, and the whale wanted to become rid of him".[199]

2.2. Alexander Deeg has stated: „Das Ziel einer Predigt müsste es sein, die Erfahrungen, die sich in den Worten des Psalms ausdrücken, für die Hörerinnen und Hörer zu eröffnen und ein Mitsprechen zu ermöglichen: Die Predigt zu Jona 2 könnte in das gemeinsame Gebet des Psalms münden." / "The aim of a sermon should be, to open the experiences which are said in the words of the psalm. All who hear these words should be ready to speak them by themselves: The sermon to Jonah 2 could guide into the common prayer of the psalm."[200] We recognize that this psalm does not refer to a special person but is for all of us!

2.3. But before we can think about the consequences for us, we have to understand this situation as one, which guides us to the death situation of Jesus of Nazareth, the Christ. That this psalm can be used as one, which gives words about the death situation of Christ, we have to see clearly. That means: That this text belongs to the Holy Saturday. This we also can see in the early Christian use:

Maybe near the end of the second half of the 3. century after Christ artists have painted this symbol in the Priscilla-Catacomb in Rom:

(This photo was taken on March 3rd, 2019.)[201]

---

[199] Cf.: https://www.rtl.de/cms/wal-verschluckt-taucher..., read on March 24th, 2019.
[200] Alexander Deeg: Die neuen alttestamentlichen Perikopentexte, p. 229 (the translation into English by myself).
[201] See: V. Nicolai, F. Bisconti and D. Mazzoleni: Roms Christliche Katakomben. Geschichte – Bilderwelt – Inschriften, Regensburg 1998, p. 100

The sea monster is swallowing out Jonah, and this is a symbol for the resurrected Jesus Christ! This conviction guides us directly to our Bible word! I have the feeling that two statements were important that the Early Church – also the Evangelist Matthew – had seen a relation to Christ:

> "[…] out of the belly of Sheol
> [the translation of the Septuagint has: "of the Hades"]
> I cried" (verse 2).
>
> And: "Deliverance belongs to the Lord" (verse 9).

The term "deliverance" guides us to that one, whose name is: "he will save his people". This means: J^{e}hoschu^{c}a = Jesus (Matthew 1:21). Therefore, this Evangelist has spoken in his Gospel about this "Sign of Jonah": "[…] but no sign shall be given to it except the sign of the prophet Jonah. […] and behold, something greater than Jonah is here" (Matthew 12:39b.41c).

I cannot really explain her the picture of "He descended to the death". Only some aspects I want to mention: „Die frühe Kirche wollte mit diesem Satz sagen, Christus ist zwischen Tod und Auferstehung dort hinabgestiegen, wo die Vergangenheit der Menschen aufbewahrt ist und hat dort die Gefangenen befreit. Die Menschheitsgeschichte hat in Christus nicht nur ein neues Ziel, sondern auch einen neuen Anfang genommen. […] Nun ist die Vergangenheit selbst verändert. Wir können uns mit ihr versöhnen. Sie kann uns helfen. Sie bindet uns nicht mehr." / "With this sentence the early church wanted to say, that Christ between death and resurrection went down there, where the past of the people is stored – and liberated the prisoners there. The history of humankind has found in Christ not only a new aim, but also a new beginning. Now the past is changed. We are redeemed with it. It may help us. We are really liberated."[202]

---

[202] That's a quote by Jörg Zink, but I do not find the source.

(I photographed this Ikon on September 21st, 2017. But I had bought it years ago in Jerusalem.)

I only want to remind the Orthodox Icon of Easter, about his work in the kingdom of death: Christ stands on the two door leaves of this kingdom of death and carries as symbols for the whole humankind Eve and Adam out of the death!

2.4. Against this background of the way of Christ, we can try to use this faith for the understanding of our human existence, better: of our Christian existence: I look into the "Apology of the Augsburg Confession": Under the headline „Frieden des Gewissens nicht durch Werke, sondern nur durch Glauben" / "Peace for the Conscience not through deeds but through faith" in chapter 50 is confessed: „Und Jona sagt Kapitel 2[,9]: »Die sich halten an das Nichtige, verlassen ihre Gnade.« Das heißt: Alles Vertrauen ist vergeblich, mit Ausnahme des Vertrauens auf die Barmherzigkeit. Die Barmherzigkeit bewahrt uns; eigene Werke, eigene Unternehmungen bewahren uns nicht. […] Deshalb geben uns nicht die Werke ruhige Gewissen, sondern die durch den Glauben ergriffene Barmherzigkeit" / "And Jonah says in chapter 2[:8]: »Those who pay regard to vain idols forsake their true loyalty." This means: All trust is meaningless, except the trust in the compassion. The compassion takes care of us, the own deeds, the own works do not care of us. […] Therefore, not our works give us calm conscience, but the compassion we have grasped by faith."[203]

---

[203] See: Unser Glaube, p. 172 (the translation into English is by myself).

May I add some strophes of one very well-known hymn:

"Amazing grace, how sweet the sound that saved a wretch like me.
I once was lost but now I am found, was blind, but now I see.

'Twas grace that taught my heart to fear, and grace my fears relieved;
How precious did that grace appear the hour I first believed.

How sweet the name of Jesus sounds in a believer's ear.
It soothes his sorrows, heals the wounds, and drives away his fear.

[…]

Through many dangers, toils and snares, I have already come;
'tis grace that brought me safe thus far, and grace will lead me home."

References:

Alexander Deeg, Andreas Schüle: Die neuen alttestamentlichen Perikopentexte. Exegetische und homiletisch-liturgische Zugänge, Leipzig ²2018: Ostermontag/Osterwoche (Reihe IV): Jona 2:(1-2)3-10(11), p. 227-229 (Alexander Deeg),
I. Sonntag nach Trinitatis (Reihe III): Jona 1:1 – 2:2(3-10)11, p. 307-310 (Andreas Schüle), p. 310-312 (Alexander Deeg),
II. Sonntag nach Trinitatis (Reihe IV): Jona 3, p. 313-315 (Andreas Schüle), p. 316-318 (Alexander Deeg).
Ernst Axel Knauf: Jona, in: Thomas Römer, Jean-Daniel Macchi, Christophe Nihan (Ed.): Einleitung in das Alte Testament. Die Bücher der Hebräischen Bibel und die alttestamentlichen Schriften der katholischen, protestantischen und orthodoxen Kirchen, Zürich 2013, p. 474-475.
Rainer Stahl: „Hinabgestiegen in das Reich des Todes", Biblical meditation to the Holy Saturday, April, 11ᵗʰ, 1998, Church of the Augustinian Order, Erfurt.
Frank Ueberschaer: Das Buch Ben Sira. Zur gegenwärtigen Forschung, ThLZ 145 (2020), cl. 897-912.
Unser Glaube. Die Bekenntnisschriften der evangelisch-lutherischen Kirche, Gütersloh ⁶2013: Die Apologie der Augsburger Konfession, p. 170-172.

Scriptures Index

1 Corinthians, 66, 72
4Q521, 34
Acts, 33, 109
Daniel, 41, 42, 43, 44, 45, 59, 78
Deuteronomy, 63, 64, 71, 72, 82
Ecclesiastes, 27, 28
Ephesians, 50
Exodus, 6, 10, 13, 20, 71, 111, 113
Ezekiel, 4, 53, 54, 55, 78, 116, 117, 118, 119
Genesis, 18, 70, 82, 86, 87
Hosea, 120
Isaiah, 8, 18, 37, 40, 41, 47, 48, 49, 50, 68, 78, 97, 117
James, 66, 73, 74, 121

Jeremiah 4, 12, 13
Jesus Sirach, 78, 120
John, 18, 57, 58, 66, 67, 69, 76, 118
Jonah, 120, 121, 122, 123, 124
1 King, 68
Leviticus, 16, 63, 117
Luke, 11, 12, 32, 50, 53, 54, 57, 58, 59, 60, 65, 66, 68, 81, 88, 109
Mark, 16, 62, 63, 65
Matthew, 17, 31, 38, 40, 41, 44, 45, 51, 52, 58, 60, 67, 70, 88, 118, 123
Numbers, 4, 21, 22, 23, 24, 25, 26
Psalm, 35, 36, 37, 49, 94, 98
Revelation, 118, 119
Romans, 11, 82, 84, 85, 109

Index of Illustrations

Paintings of the Cathedral in Nuremberg	14, 114
Mosaics of the Cathedral in Saint Petersburg	14, 88
Ikon of the Trinity, Samara	18
The not with human hand painted picture	19
Christmas in Singapore, 1984	48
Pictures by Uriel Birnbaum	112
Fresco in Dura Europos	117
Fresco of the Priscilla-Catacomb	122
Ikon of Easter	124